THE PHARAOHS' CODE

CREATING A JOYFUL LIFE AND A LASTING LEGACY

Mohamed Tohami

ISBN: 1-4392-1242-2
ISBN-13: 9781439212424

Visit www.booksurge.com to order additional copies.

Praise for *The Pharaohs' Code*

"*The Pharaohs' Code* is essential reading for every person whose goals go beyond simple success to the loftier heights of leaving a lasting legacy. Tohami's book is motivating, inspiring, and full of practical wisdom that is transformational. By following the processes in this book, you'll discover how to experience more joy in your life and succeed beyond your imagination."

—Dr. Tony Alessandra
Bestselling author of *The Platinum Rule* and *Charisma*

"As a bestselling author of self-help and personal development books, I know just how difficult it is to put pen to paper and try to transform readers' lives in the process. Thank you, Tohami! You have quite successfully done this in your brilliant new book release, *The Pharaoh's Code: Creating a Joyful Life and a Lasting Legacy*.

Tohami's book not only underscores a life-altering process for finding your passion, but offers the wisdom of the Pharaohs and their inspirational proverbs which will guide you on your path to creating your ultimate legacy. I have written and spoken extensively on the power of one's soul print. This book is more than a process, it is a soul print that will leave you with a long-lasting approach to activating your greater potential and true happiness. *The Pharaohs' Code* is not just a success journey, it is a critical and necessary expedition we all need to take if we are to achieve greater authenticity and everlasting success and personal fulfillment in life. The expedition starts here, with this amazing book."

—Anne Bruce
International speaker and trainer
Bestselling author of *Discover True North*,
Be Your Own Mentor, and *Speak for a Living*

"*The Pharaohs' Code* by Mohamed Tohami is a book filled with essential success principles that you will want to study and master to achieve overwhelming success, no matter what you define that to be...but it's also much more. The book is a roadmap for living your best life—a life filled with meaning, contribution, passion, and joy, and a life worth living while leaving a legacy for generations to come, just as the Pharaohs did. It is wise, inspirational, and insightful and I give it my highest recommendation."

—Dr. Joe Rubino
Founder, CenterForPersonalReinvention.com
Creator, SelfEsteemSystem.com

"In his new book *The Pharaohs' Code: Creating a Joyful Life and a Lasting Legacy*, Mohamed Tohami has brilliantly combined the ancient teachings of his native Egypt with top-of-the-line tools and applications for creating a life of empowerment, passion, and potential in today's world. Tohami blends the philosophies of then and now—showing us all how there is truly only one timeless Universe—into dynamic, easy-to-follow steps for changing our lives and fulfilling our dreams today. Part education, part workbook, and totally motivating, **The Pharaohs' Code** lays the seeds you will need for a new, expanded, and joy-filled pathway. This is a read you won't want to miss!"

—Sandy Brewer
Author of *Pursuit of Light: An Extraordinary Journey*

"Motivating, inspiring, and full of wisdom. *The Pharaohs' Code* reveals a unique approach that crosses cultures and is for anyone who wants to live with passion and make a difference. I loved it!"

—Brian Klemmer
Bestselling author of *The Compassionate Samurai*

ISIS TEMPLE IN PHILAE, EGYPT

I dedicate this book to you and to all seekers who have an intense desire to find joy in their lives and, with their legacies, to live on in the hearts and minds of others for years to come.

Acknowledgments

My editor, Renée LaTulippe, has been my secret weapon throughout the process of bringing this book into existence. Her amazing work has really given life and breath to my words and ideas. She has been vital to the quality of this book. Tarek Zaki has been so helpful with the information resources he referred me to in my research on the lifestyle and wisdom of the Pharaohs. Mahmoud Helmy, my wonderful and supportive friend, believed in me every single moment of my journey. My parents have given me support and brought me up to where I am now. And special thanks to my loving partner, Esraa Amer, who has given me her beautiful love and support.

I'm grateful to all who have supported me in this exciting journey and give thanks to God who showers me with his blessings all the time.

Table of Contents

Foreword by Jim Cathcart

Foreword

By Jim Cathcart
Bestselling author of *The Acorn Principle*

You can usually expect a foreword to be an endorsement of the author or the data in the book. And, yes, I certainly want to offer my support to Mohamed Tohami and his words. But more than that I want to endorse his system. In *The Pharaohs' Code* you are introduced to a series of actions that, once applied, will truly transform your life.

I know this because I have done these steps personally and the result has been a rewarding career that now exceeds thirty-one years. When I started on the quest that you will follow here, I was a government clerk in Little Rock, Arkansas in the United States. My job title was Assistant Loan Specialist—and the Loan Specialist was not a busy man!

In other words, I had an unnecessary job at a low wage and found very little satisfaction in my daily work. Though the workload was light, I found myself dreading each day's work. Not the effort, but the sense of waste. I found my role almost meaningless and somewhat depressing.

In an effort to distract myself, I read books all day, wrote about my dreams in a journal, and listened to the radio.

Then one day I heard a short radio broadcast by Earl Nightingale, a man known as the "Dean of Personal Motivation." When I heard this particular broadcast in 1972, his show was already on over nine hundred radio stations around the world. That day he said, "If you spend one extra hour each day in study in your chosen field, you will become a national expert in that field in five years or less."

I was stunned. Only one extra hour a day? I had eight extra hours each day due to my meaningless job. So I took up his challenge and started wondering, "What do I want to become an expert at?" The longer I thought the clearer it became that I wanted to do what Earl Nightingale was doing. I wanted to help people grow. But I had a problem—not only had I never given a speech, I also had nothing to say!

So I started studying personal development materials: books, recordings, seminars, experts, leaders, any source I could find. I became fanatical about it. It's all I wanted to think and talk about. Some of my friends drifted away because my interests were now different from theirs. New friends emerged. We became fellow students and collaborated often. I joined the Junior Chamber of Commerce (the Jaycees) and started getting very active in community service projects. I learned to set goals, assess my skills, use my strengths, gain the support of others, develop plans, communicate persuasively, and more.

In two short years I attended over four hundred Jaycees meetings and events. I became a chapter leader, then a state leader, and then a national leader. I spent 1974 working as a representative of Earl Nightingale's company and selling his training programs. Then in 1975 the United States Jaycees hired me to be the senior program manager in charge of individual development programs at their national headquarters. I was now a national expert on personal development! (At least I was when compared to my position when I first heard that radio broadcast.)

After two years on their national staff and much travel to deliver speeches and promote the use of our training materials, I went out on my own as a speaker and trainer.

By maintaining the discipline and aggressive study in my field, I continued to advance. Then, in 1984 as I sat in my corporate offices in La Jolla, California, my phone rang. It was Earl Nightingale calling to speak with me! He wanted to publish my materials on personal development. I, of course, agreed.

My audio album entitled "Relationship Strategies," which was co-authored with Dr. Tony Alessandra, was published by Nightingale-Conant Corporation in 1984. And in the first two years they sold more than 3.5 million dollars worth of albums. In 1974 I was selling Earl Nightingale's recordings and in 1984 he was selling mine!

This system works! I've seen it work for thousands of people and I know it will work for you. Follow the wisdom of the pharaohs and the guidance of Mohamed Tohami. Your life will be more rewarding and meaningful because of it.

Live a life of joy and of meaning. Leave a legacy.

In the Spirit of Growth,
Jim Cathcart

STATUES OF PHARAOH RAMSES II AND QUEEN NEFERTARI
FACING A GOLDEN SUNRISE AT THE ENTRANCE OF
ABU SIMBEL TEMPLE

Introduction
Success vs. Everlasting Success

"Success is not final, failure is not fatal: it is the courage to continue that counts."

—Winston Churchill

Hello from Egypt, **the Land of Pharaohs and the Cradle of Civilization!**

Our culture is steeped in history. Everywhere you travel, you are reminded of the great legacies left behind by our pharaoh forefathers. Abundant legacies of success surround us. The Great Pyramids, the Sphinx, and the grand temples built by wealthy, successful pharaohs are a daily reminder of what each of our lives can be. Not just in Egypt, but anywhere in the world.

This culture has inspired me since my childhood and has guided me to start uncovering the Ancient Egyptian secrets that bring joy, wealth, and everlasting success. And I want to help you explore the many possibilities that lay in front of you—possibilities for greatness. Possibilities for everlasting success.

But before we start, let me tell you a shocking truth:

SUCCESS IS NOT ENOUGH

Have you ever heard about people who achieved huge success in a short period of time? Have you ever dreamed of being like them? And while you were dreaming of being like them, did you then discover that they suddenly lost everything? How many times have you seen people become shining stars in their fields only to be forgotten a few years later?

As a result of hearing about such experiences, perhaps you developed a strong belief that having an average life is much better than facing such immense failure. And so you accepted your pain, lost your true power, hid your potential, lived an unbalanced life, never did what you love to do, and never felt satisfied. The list of "nevers" could go on and on, right?

That list of "nevers" is exactly why it is not enough to just succeed or even to learn about how to succeed. It is much more important for you to learn

HOW TO CREATE EVERLASTING SUCCESS.

So what's the difference between "regular" success and everlasting success? Why is the latter so much more important? There are several reasons:

- It is the kind of success that never vanishes.
- It allows you to live the most satisfying life of your dreams.
- It allows you to reveal your true value.
- It allows you to see failure as your friend and best teacher and to see challenges as opportunities.
- It allows you to be remembered after you pass away.

Do you agree that *you* deserve that kind of success?

Anyone can tell you that achieving initial success is easy. The most difficult part in the success equation, however, is the continuity—that is, maintaining the success you reach and continuing to grow it. It doesn't matter how many failures you face during the journey; the most important thing is to end your life with a grand finale—to end it with an ultimate legacy.

I imagine you'd agree with me in thinking how disappointing and sad it would be to be like one of those people who looks wealthy and happy on the outside, but yet still chooses to end his life in suicide. In the final years, he realizes that he has lived a meaningless life and was never fulfilled.

Fail as much as you want because failure is your best teacher—as long as you learn the lesson and move forward, of course. Just develop the habit of recognizing the lesson and cultivating the belief that failure is not fatal.

As long as you're still breathing there is another chance to succeed. The moment you decide to quit is the moment you really fail. For me, failure is an illusion. It doesn't mean anything except that you're still lacking some lessons that will help you take your life to the next level. The role of failure is to build you up and shape your character until you deserve to occupy your desired level of success.

Who on earth doesn't fail?

We all fail. The most important thing is knowing how to face and handle failure, and how to use it as a stepping stone to reach your goals and dreams. If you succeed, that is a good thing. But the best lessons you learn in life come from your failures. Socrates used a similar philosophy in regards to marriage: "If a man has a good marriage, that is a good thing. If he has a bad marriage, he becomes a philosopher, and that is a good thing." That is a truly amazing philosophy. It teaches you how to handle both success and failure.

When you succeed, it is good—congratulations! You need to spend some time analyzing your success to understand its key lessons so that you can repeat them again and again to achieve future successes.

And when you fail, you need to spend almost three times as much time analyzing your failure to understand its key lessons. The fact is that successful people are the ones who fail the most. If you don't fail, then you aren't growing. If you don't fail, then you aren't doing something worthy. After all, the best lessons you can learn in your life come from your failures.

So from now on, be an analyst. Don't let your successes and failures pass without analyzing them for the lessons they offer—then learn how to grow and expand from those lessons and take that knowledge with you to the next level. Doing so will make you a philosopher, a wise man, and a good student of life. The lessons you learn from your own life experiences are much more powerful than those you read in a book or hear in a speech. And remember that continuity is the essence of everlasting success. The pharaohs built a legacy that still impresses us and left secrets that are still undiscovered. Focus on building your own everlasting success. Create something that shows the world the value of who you truly are. Give back the magnificence of your creation. You're a miracle and you must leave a miracle. Be a legend with a legacy that makes this world a better place for generations to come. Be the light that guides others in dark times, the hope that inspires in desperate times, and the fire that empowers in times of weakness. Strive to transform your life from making a living to making a difference.

Today is the first day of the rest of your life!

Today is a new day. Don't look back. The past has passed. Today is all you have, so live it in the best way possible. If you are still allowing your past to shape your future, then you must stop that immediately. Failing in the past doesn't necessarily mean that you are going to fail in the future. Being poor in the past doesn't necessarily mean that you will continue to be poor. Whatever your life looked like in the past, it doesn't mean that that is how your future must be. You have the power to change your direction instantly and move in the path that will lead you to the destination of your dreams.

The most important thing is to select the right path; otherwise, you will ruin your future and end up with nothing but disappointment and dissatisfaction. Choose your path carefully and start pursuing your dreams with faith and passion. You have unlimited potential. Don't let the past hinder you from reaching your full potential. Remember that your future mostly depends on your present, not on your past.

Look at today as a new birth of your soul, a new birth of your heart, and a new birth of your mind. What you do today and every day from now on will determine your future. Act as if you've already achieved your dreams. Be the person you want to be. Live your dream in your mind and prepare for its manifestation in your life. You were meant to live in great abundance. Start today, with the help of this book, to pursue your dreams. Take one more step every day and let the law of accumulation work for you. You were born to live a great life, a life in which you embrace your unique values and make your maximum contribution.

Today is the first day of the rest of your extraordinary life!

And now let's move on to The Pharaohs' Code.

Section 1:
The Pharaohs' Code

EGYPTIAN PAPYRUS SHOWING THE LAST JUDGMENT. IF
YOUR HEART IS LIGHTER THAN THE FEATHER,
YOU MAY ENTER PARADISE.

Chapter 1
Afterlife!

> *Did you find joy in your life?*
> *Did your life bring joy to others?*

Religion guided every aspect of ancient Egyptian life. From the earliest times, the Egyptians paid homage to their dead by burying them and shielding their remains for eternity. Their view of the afterlife was highly developed, as evidenced by the elaborate rituals for preparing the body and soul for a peaceful life after death. The Egyptians also saw death as a transitional stage in the journey to a better life in the next world. They believed that they could only reach their full potential after death. Like many cultures, the ancient Egyptians were driven to find meaning in existence.

These beliefs are beautifully portrayed in a scene from the movie *The Bucket List*.

Edward Cole (Jack Nicholson), a pursuer of wealth, and Carter Chambers (Morgan Freeman), a brilliant auto mechanic who seems to know the answer to every question, find themselves in the same boat when they are both diagnosed with terminal cancer. The unlikely pairing of two people on such divergent paths opens their eyes to an opportunity to evaluate who they are and to experience the change of heart they need in order to find joy in their lives.

That opportunity comes when Chambers remembers an exercise his philosophy teacher once assigned to his class. The students were to make a list of the things they wanted to do in their lives before they "kicked the bucket." Taking the assignment literally, Cole and Chambers set off on an adventure prescribed by their lists and experience life-altering transformations.

The key moment comes when they are sitting on the top of an ancient tomb in Egypt with the Great Pyramids spread before them. Chambers explains that the ancient Egyptians believed that when one enters the afterlife, the custodians of the gate ask two questions to decide who is qualified for heaven:

> *Did you find joy in your life?*
> *Did your life bring joy to others?*

That is The Pharaohs' Code!

It is fairly easy to understand that finding the joy in your life has nothing to do with money or intellect. Finding joy has everything to do with your heart being reconnected to what you truly love to do and to those who want to share your love. That is a worthy goal for all of us to accomplish before that final bucket is kicked.

It is neither good to live for yourself alone nor to live for others alone. Balance in everything is the essence of successful living. Enjoy life and help others do the same. The best approach you can follow is to start with *yourself*. When you are joyful you can help others be joyful. The concept is simple—in order to help others feel or reach a certain emotion or status, you must first experience that emotion or status yourself. A poor man can't help others become wealthy! So start by finding the joy in your own life and then look for ways to help others find their joy. When you succeed in bringing joy to others, it will come back to you tenfold, and then the cycle continues. You get ready, you give, you receive, and then you give more and receive more.

I invite you to live life to the fullest and maximize your experience. This is the only way you can help others. The most satisfying feeling you can ever have is when you see that you've created a legacy that helps thousands of people grow and prosper over the years.

Stand Up for Your Dreams

When you were a child, you dared to dream anything. Nothing was impossible. It doesn't matter whether you had big dreams, small dreams, or crazy dreams. What matters most is that you had the *power to dream*. Look at how you are now. Do you still have the power to dream? Or have your dreams died? Are you playing it safe? Do you compromise your happiness and accept being among average people who know neither victory nor defeat? Are you living with people who spend their lives in the gray area?

Here is the undeniable fact:

All successful people are big dreamers.

To succeed in life you *must* have a dream. You can't live without a purpose that gives your life meaning and joy. Let me tell you the *truth*—you have to either *dream* or *regret*. Yes, regret! Someday you will lie on your deathbed and look back at your past. If you had no dreams, you will regret your meaningless life and wish for another chance to live your life again and to *dream big*. Mohamed Ali once said: "The one without dreams is the one without wings." The world needs you, so aim for the top.

What are your wildest dreams? Set aside some time today and bring those dreams back to life. Dream, set goals, develop a plan, and *take action now*. Remember, dream or regret—which one are you going to choose?

My brother/sister in humanity, I implore you to do three things:

Stand up for your dreams.
Stand up for your greatness.
Stand up for your legacy.

You've got it within yourself to create an amazing life. Dig deeper within yourself and search for your dreams, for your unique purpose in life.

Don't let your fears kick in. Rebuff the naysayers and say to yourself, "I can do it." Set your sights for the top of the mountain and *stand up for your dreams.*

When you get to the end of your life, you want to know that you did all that you could to make this world a better place and to improve the lives of millions of people around the world. You want to know that you've awakened giants. You want to know that you gave your life your best shot. My friend, *you* can make a difference.

As you read through this book, I'm going to show you how to follow The Pharaohs' Code to find the joy in your life, bring joy to others, and create your ultimate legacy. I'll walk you through an exciting journey toward a meaningful life that is full of purpose, passion, and satisfaction. It's time to ask yourself these two significant questions:

- Do I find joy in my life?
- Does my life bring joy to others?

Chapter 2
The Lost Emotion

"You will free yourself when you learn to be neutral and follow the instructions of your heart without letting things perturb you."
—Ancient Egyptian proverb written
on the Pharaohs' temples in Luxor

Through my personal experience, my research, and the interviews I've conducted with over one hundred ultra-successful people, I have discovered that there is a single lost emotion responsible for *all* great success stories in the history of mankind.

That lost emotion is <u>passion</u>.

The world moves very fast these days and the hectic pace of life forces most people to fight for shelter and security, trapping them into just making a living and fighting for survival. And once people are trapped, they start saying they're "sick and tired of being sick and tired."

The constant stress of modern life has overshadowed the importance of this one emotion, and its loss has taken more lives than all the wars in the history of the world—but the biggest tragedy is that its loss has taken the lives of people who are still breathing. Yes, the loss of that one emotion has turned people into zombies. They may be alive physiologically, but their hearts and their passion for life were lost long ago. And the world has become more violent since the loss of this emotion. People are disconnected from one another, focused exclusively on their own lives and on how to survive. The focus of everyday life has shifted from *service* to *survival*.

The path of mankind is congested with people who enter and exit the world without so much as leaving a smudge on the pages of history, whereas others manage to create everlasting success and, through their legacies, live on in the hearts and minds of those who come after them. Those shining stars excelled because they embraced the lost emotion and incorporated it into every single moment of their lives.

The day I discovered that lost emotion inside of me and started pumping it into every area of my life, everything changed for me and I experienced a complete life makeover.

Only When You Breathe It In Can the Transformation Begin

When I was seventeen years old, I started searching for what I really wanted to do with my life. I didn't want to live an ordinary life. I didn't want to go to college, get a boring dead-end job, get married, and keep working...at that boring dead-end job... just to pay the bills and barely support my family. No! I wanted more out of life!

Don't get me wrong—there's nothing wrong with going to college, getting a good job, and getting married. But I wanted to give my family everything they deserved, all the wonderful things life has to offer—*and* I wanted to be fulfilled while I was doing it. I wanted to live my dream, enjoy what I was doing with my life, and make enough money to live...not to get by, but to really *live!* Most importantly, my friend, I wanted to find a way to serve others and make a difference.

So I started reading all the books about success and personal development that I could get my hands on. And I attended as many courses and seminars as I possibly could. I believed so much in the power of human potential and in what a person can achieve if he has a dream and a clear purpose in life. One day, after six years of searching, I discovered the giant inside of me. At last, I had found the meaning of my life. And in the process I found a way to contribute to other people's lives. From that moment I started doing things I would never have been able to do before.

My life transformation began when I slowly started to venture out of the cocoon of the ordinary and began to explore the realm of the extraordinary. It began when I reclaimed the joy of waking up every morning, full of energy and exhilaration. *It began with the birth of The Lost Emotion,* the most powerful transformational life force of all ages. It began when I found my *passion* and decided to *live* it.

Don't Settle for a Good Life—Only a Spectacular One!

Most of us just hope to live a good life: to have a nice family, to raise good kids, to have a decent job. But greatness and the creation of everlasting success begin when you aspire to live a spectacular life. A life that makes an impact and leaves a legacy. A life that gets you out of the cocoon of the ordinary and into the realm of the extraordinary. A life that ensures you are remembered after you pass away.

We are born to succeed and make a difference. We have a mission to accomplish from the moment we enter into life. That mission is to make the world a better place to live in. That mission is to make a difference that will positively impact thousands, even millions of people. That mission is to serve and cultivate value that will benefit the generations to come. Don't ever settle for a good life—only a spectacular one. Make the decision today and I guarantee that if you are committed to it, you will experience a complete life makeover. And if you want to live your ideal life then there is only one answer: *live with passion*. The path to success is the path paved with passion.

Now, you may ask: "What about the problems that I might face along the way?" And the answer is simple: "They don't matter!"

Why?

Because your *own* passion is the ultimate motivation you need to achieve your dreams and aspirations, and living with passion is the core of a fulfilled life. Following your heart will turn your life into a satisfying masterpiece. Acting on your passions will help you create a legacy that will remain in the hearts and memories of others for years to come.

Give yourself permission to *be unique*. Liberate your uniqueness, see your life with your own eyes, and live it with your own heart. Build your own vision of your ideal life, follow your passion, and craft your ultimate legacy. After all, your life does not belong to other people—it is yours alone. And did I mention that it is very short? So take action today and take advantage of all the precious moments of your life. Don't live it small—live it *big* and make an impact on the world.

Education vs. Passion

"Are you crazy?"

"Do you want to throw five years of engineering education in the wastebasket just to follow what you call your passion?"

"Forget about it. You'll never make it."

"You're qualified as an engineer and that is what you should do for the rest of your life."

"Don't waste five years of education, my dear."

Can you relate to these declarations? These bits of "wisdom" that other people call "advice"? That was the first challenge I faced when I started following my passion and living my true purpose in life. This is what I heard from my parents, my friends, and my family. Sure, they were all just trying to give me their honest advice, but they didn't realize that there is only one path to success—and that is the path of passion! The biggest challenge for me was figuring out how to start from scratch in a field that I knew nothing about. Could I do it just because I loved it? Would that work? Was it possible? Did I really waste five years of education? Should I continue on that path just because I already spent five years of my life following it? Let me tell you this bluntly, based on my experience and the point I've reached now, after boldly following my passion:

Fact #1: You can neglect five years of education—it's better than neglecting the rest of your life. Five years shouldn't determine or destroy the entire course of your life.

Fact #2: You only excel at what you love to do. Education won't make you excellent.

Fact #3: Education won't provide you satisfaction. Satisfaction only comes from your heart, by following your passion.

Fact #4: Your past should never control your future. As Stephen Covey, the bestselling author of *The 7 Habits of Highly Effective People*, says: "Live out of your imagination, not your history."

Fact #5: All great people achieved massive success because they followed their passion and their spiritual impulse.

Fact #6: Your true purpose in life is where your maximum passion lies. You can only embrace your life and get the most out of it if you follow your unique purpose. Otherwise, you just live a half-hearted, meaningless life.

Fact #7: I have never achieved greater levels of success and satisfaction than I did when I simply followed my passion. And I did it faster than I would have if I had taken any other path. In just five years, I became an internationally recognized success expert. And yes, I started without any previous knowledge or education.

How Successful People Defend Their Dreams

Sometimes I really wish I could become deaf and blind to all the naysayers and negative people who seem to want to sabotage my dreams and stand in the way of my goals. Don't you? The people who surround you, even the closest ones, can often be the hardest obstacle to overcome on your way to fulfilling your desires and living the life of your dreams. Why? Because people who aspire to massive success are often seen as a threat to the average person, and those average people may unconsciously—or consciously—try to pull those ambitious people down to their level so that they are not left behind to suffer a mediocre life alone.

How many times have you been criticized or subjected to rejection or ridicule? What did you do in those situations? If your normal reaction is to stop what you are doing, to halt your own progress in order to focus on defending yourself or trying to prove your point, then *stop*. That is a waste of your time and effort. Life is too short and too valuable to throw it away on such nonsense. One thing you can be sure about is that you will never please everyone; no one can, so why bother trying?

You have a dream and a unique mission on this earth that only you can fulfill. Discover what it is and give it all you've got. Give it your time, energy, and focus. Believe in it and move forward. How people see you is irrelevant and has nothing to do with you or your dream of success. I am not saying that you shouldn't listen to good advice, of course. Just be mindful of what kind of advice you're receiving and from whom you're receiving it. Take what can really improve your progress and help you along your journey, but never pay attention to negative people who are *not* successful and are *not* living the kind of worthy life you aim for. Take advice from people who are already successful, know how to overcome challenges, and can guide you with their experience and knowledge. That is the kind of advice that you need to pay attention to.

Why on earth should you listen to someone who is living a mediocre life with no meaning or purpose? A phrase I read in Paulo Coelho's *The Witch of Portobello* really sums up the point: "You either carry your mission forward or you can defend yourself. You're aware, I know, that what you're doing is more important than how you're seen by other people. Do you agree?"

What you're doing is more important than how you're seen by other people. So carry on with your mission, keep moving forward, and let your legacy speak for itself. Successful people know that their mission is greater and more important than other people's opinions. So never let the naysayers pull you down and never kill your dreams to please other people. When it comes to your mission and your dream, it's a good practice to become deaf and blind to negative forces and to open your mind to the valuable advice of successful people who have been where you are and know the art of success.

Keep moving forward and craft your legacy, and someday the impact of your mission will leave all those who stood against you absolutely speechless. Attacking, not defending, is the best way to win the game of life.

Passion performs miracles, my friend. Don't let anything or anyone override your passion. Passion gives you a beautiful sense of joy, freedom, satisfaction, and meaning. To achieve massive success, you just need a passion that is much more powerful than all your fears and all that the naysayers tell you. Unleash your passion and feel the power of an enlightened life.

When you understand that passion is the key to living your ideal life, you will be ready to take the first step toward success.

> *"Follow your passion and you'll find the joy in your life!*
> *Only when you breathe it in can the transformation begin."*
> —Mohamed Tohami

Chapter 3
Know Yourself

"The kingdom of heaven is within you; and whosoever shall know himself shall find it."

—Ancient Egyptian proverb written
on the Pharaohs' temples in Luxor

One of the main religious concepts of the ancient Egyptians was "know thyself." Their spiritual aspect of this concept held that within man is the divine essence of the Creator and the Heavens. And this finds expression in their teaching: "The kingdom of heaven is within you; and whosoever shall know himself shall find it."

The "know yourself" concept is also one of Socrates' most famous quotes, a quote that literally summarizes in just two words the way a person can unleash his full potential and achieve success. The more you know about yourself, the more you can achieve. If you don't know yourself really well, you'll end up limiting yourself by playing it safe—and in doing so, you'll waste 95% of your true potential.

Do you know how powerful you are? Don't just look at who you are right now, look at who you can be! You're one of God's most magnificent creatures. You have a brain with fantastic powers and potential. Just think—despite the greatest advancements in biology and anatomy, scientists have only just begun to discover the true capabilities of the brain. Did you know that:

- Einstein's brain was of average size.
- Your heart beats 101,000 times a day.
- 50,000 of the cells in your body will die and be replaced by new cells in the time it takes you to read this sentence!

- In one hour, your heart works hard enough to produce the equivalent energy to raise almost one ton of weight one yard off the ground.
- In one square inch of skin there are four yards of nerve fibers, 1300 nerve cells, 100 sweat glands, three million cells, and three yards of blood vessels.
- There are 45 miles of nerves in a human being.
- One human brain generates more electrical impulses in a single day than all of the world's telephones put together.
- If your entire DNA was stretched out, it would reach to the moon 6000 times.
- The muscle that controls the blinking of your eye is the fastest muscle in your body.
- Behind the iris of your eye is a soft, rubbery lens that focuses light onto the retina. The retina contains about 125 million rods and seven million cones. The rods pick up shades of gray and help us see in dim light; the cones work best in bright light to pick up colors.
- We actually do not see with our eyes, but with our brains. The eyes are basically the cameras of the brain.
- One-quarter of the brain is used to control the eyes.

And that's just to mention a few of the facts scientists have discovered so far. And then you hear people say, "I can't." Throw the word "can't" in the trash can! Burn it, bury it, and forget about it *forever*. With all your miracles, how on earth can you say you "can't"? If you can't, then who can?

Look inside yourself and you'll find one miracle after another. With all that potential and all those capabilities, why are you limiting yourself? Know who you truly are and you will soon understand what you can achieve. All you have to do is believe in yourself. Know your values and beliefs. Know your talents and passions. Know your true purpose and what you're meant to do in this life. Know your strengths as well as your weaknesses. Know yourself. You live with yourself more than you live with anyone else. Don't you think you should know everything about your everlasting partner?

Know Who You Want to Be

One day I was watching a video by Jim Cathcart, business author and one of the top twenty speakers in the world. He was sharing some secrets and principles to help sales people maintain the right attitude. During his speech, Jim shared a very powerful question that created a true mind shift for me: "How would the person you want to be do the things you are about to do?" Amazing, right?

That question puts you in a position in the future where you are the ideal person you would like to be, and helps you act from that perspective in your present life. That simple question activates the power of the "act as if" principle. You act as if you have already reached your goals and have become the person you always wanted to be. "Acting as if" will focus your mind and shape your thoughts around your ultimate dream. Acting as if you've reached your goals will also shape your character in the best and fastest way possible. You will immediately start "modeling" your ideal self, which will help you develop and maintain a success mindset—and a positive attitude—every moment of your life. If you are not already acting as if you have succeeded and using the qualities that are required to reach your goal, you will hinder your chances to succeed. Thinking about how the person you would like to be would act in a certain situation will help you choose the most powerful actions that will get you to where you want to be in less time.

The Obvious Truth about Getting What You Want in Life

"I wish to be successful."
"I wish to get promoted."
"I wish to lose weight."
"I wish to get rich."

In *As a Man Thinketh*, James Allen wrote: "Not what he wishes and prays for does a man get, but what he justly earns. His wishes and prayers are only gratified and answered when they harmonize with his thoughts and actions." Fabulous! We all have wishes but, unfortunately, wishing for something is not enough.

The brilliant term "justly earns" holds the obvious truth about getting what you want in life. Most people wish for things that they are simply not qualified for—not yet, anyway. They wish to become successful, but they don't think or act like successful people. They just go through life with the same old mentality that got them to where they are today. They wish to become rich, but they have a victim mentality and think like poor people, or they think money is a big evil and they don't want or even deserve to have it. They wish to get promoted, but they are not fully qualified to take on the new position.

If you fall into these same traps, then here is a warning flag: you only get what you justly earn. I know you might say that life is not always that fair, but *that is a myth*. Life *is* fair. Yes, life is fair no matter how it may appear to you. Perhaps you've gone through some hard times and tough circumstances that made you think life is unfair. Perhaps you just didn't understand why all of these bad things were happening to you. But here is a tip that might give you a clear understanding of how life works:

> *You have to burn gold to remove the dross.*

Life "burns" you to get rid of all that dross—all the impurities, trivialities, fears, and inferior bits that are marring the surface of the shining gold that is *you*. It burns you to help you develop the qualifications you need to succeed, my friend! Your mission in life requires you to learn vital lessons that you can only learn through adversity. Tough times give you what you need to "justly earn" what you want in life.

Look at another profound thought by James Allen: "Man is buffeted by circumstances so long as he believes himself to be the creature of outside conditions. But when he realizes that he is a creative power and that he may command the hidden soil and seeds of his being out of which circumstances grow, he then becomes the rightful master of himself."

You are the master of yourself and only you are the creator of your destiny. Why? Because you are in control of your thoughts and, therefore, your actions. Your wishes and prayers are only gratified and answered when they harmonize with your thoughts and actions. Before thinking that life is unfair, first examine your thoughts and actions. Are they in harmony with the level of success you want to achieve? If yes, then rest assured that you are on the right path, and trust that God is fair—and very soon you will see the fruit of your thoughts and actions.

Stop struggling against outside influences and circumstances beyond your control. Instead, learn from all of the experiences that life throws at you, good or bad, because every situation holds a key lesson for you. Use your circumstances to discover your hidden powers. Prove that you deserve what you want before you wish to have it. Harmonize your thoughts and actions with what you wish, and see how success will naturally be attracted to you.

> *"A man only begins to be a man when he builds himself up in strong and noble thoughts; ceases to kick against circumstances, but begins to use them as aids to his more rapid progress and as a means of discovering the hidden powers and possibilities within himself."*
>
> —James Allen

The smart farmer trusts that life is fair and that the laws of nature never fail. If he nurtures good seeds, he will reap a good harvest. If he puts in the necessary effort, he will reap the expected rewards. The smart farmer does his homework: he studies the soil and the weather and plants quality seeds. You'll never see him just sitting around wishing and hoping that the earth will give him a good harvest! Follow the laws of the universe and trust that you will get what you justly earn.

Now I'm going to ask you to do two things—I promise, just two things! But in return, please promise me that you will do them. Starting today, find out more about yourself than you know about your favorite movie star. And from now on, before taking any action, ask yourself this question: "How would the person I want to be do the things I am about to do?" You're only living in this moment—why not act as if you've already realized your dreams?

Believe me, the world needs you and you can make a difference—a *big* difference. When you know who you truly are and who you want to be, you will be amazed at what you can be and do in this life. Unleash yourself! The Pharaohs' wisdom is simple. All you have to do, both now and in the future, is follow the advice of those two little words: know yourself. The kingdom of heaven is within you.

Your success is waiting just around the corner.

Chapter 4
The 10 Greatest Virtues of All

"If you would build something solid, don't work with wind: always look for a fixed point, something you know that is stable...yourself."

—Ancient Egyptian proverb written
on the Pharaohs' temples in Luxor

Ancient Egyptian priests were known as *hem-netjer* (servants of the god) and were essentially officials who were employed at the temple to look after its daily needs. There were groups of priests who had specialized knowledge, others who taught writing and copied out texts, and still others who attended to the economic organization of the temple. Temples were the residences of the gods, but the enclosure could also include workshops, libraries, and estates. As such, a priest in Ancient Egypt had a different role than a modern-day priest.

Before the priest could enter the innermost sanctuary where the god resided, he had to purify himself by performing a series of cleansing rituals. They also abstained from certain foods, although this did not involve ritual fasting. They were permitted to wear only garments of linen and white papyrus sandals. The higher ranks were favored with special robes such as leopard skins. When the priest was ready to enter the temple, he would wash himself in water to rinse away dirt and sweat and to bestow energy and rejuvenation upon himself.

The Egyptian priests took great care in the selection and acceptance of candidates into their temples. In the Egyptian Mysteries, the Neophyte was required to manifest the following attributes*:

---

* From *Stolen Legacy* by George G. M. James (pp. 30–31).

1. Control of thought
2. Control of action
3. Steadfastness of purpose
4. Evidence of having a mission in life
5. Identity with spiritual life
6. Evidence of prudence
7. Freedom from resentment
8. Confidence in the power of the master as teacher
9. Confidence in one's own ability to learn
10. Preparedness for initiation

I believe that these are the ten greatest virtues of all and I would like to examine each one in detail.

Virtue 1: Control of Thought
Virtue 2: Control of Action

If you are like most people, you might have already wasted countless hours and effort trying to change your reality, without success. The surprising truth is that when successful people want to change their reality, they focus their energy on only *one* thing—and before long, they get better results and dramatically improve every aspect of their lives. Let me show you how it's done.

First, let's take a look at the two major components that directly affect your results—your thoughts and your actions. In *As a Man Thinketh*, James Allen said that "action is the blossom of thought, and joy and suffering are its fruit." Every action you take springs directly from the seeds of your thoughts and the result you get, whether it's joy or suffering, is the fruit of your actions. Breaking this process down into its simplest form—Thought - Action - Result—leads to an inevitable and important conclusion: your thoughts are the root cause of all the results you get. Therefore, you must *change your thoughts* to change your reality.

That concept is what drives successful people into action. They know that their thoughts shape their reality and that if they want better results instantly they must fix what is broken in their *own minds*. Complaining and blaming are not a part of their world. Those successful people pluck out the thoughts that hinder them from moving forward and replace them with powerful new ones. It really is that simple—but as it's often said, common sense is not always common practice. If you know of any other formula for changing your reality, great! Do it and tell me about your results. But if you want to avoid endless hours or years of trial and error, follow the tracks that other successful people have left behind—Thought - Action - Result—and remember that only *you* have the power to change your thoughts and therefore change your reality.

> *"The plant reveals what is in the seed."*
> —Ancient Egyptian proverb written
> on the Pharaohs' temples in Luxor

This concept is a simple demonstration of the natural law of cause and effect. The cause of your reality is your thoughts. Your thoughts drive your actions, which in turn lead to the results you get. Your mind is like a garden and to reap good fruit, you must plant good seeds. That is what the smart farmer knows by nature—change the quality of the seeds and you will change the quality of the fruit. Start planting your mind with quality thoughts. Immerse yourself in the ideas of successful people and soak them up like a sponge. Before you know it, you'll practically have a brand-new life. Weed out those negative, useless thoughts and fix what's broken in your *own mind*—because your mind holds the secret key that will unlock the door to a prosperous new reality.

Does that sound easier said than done? Then let me share with you two concepts that will help you change your negative thoughts and replace them with positive ones.

Concept 1: The 4x3 Negative Thinking Crusher Process

This first concept is a proven 4-step process that will get you thinking about how you think and help you change your thought process.

Step 1: Search

Search for the dominant negative thoughts that are engraved in your mind. Dig deeply to find their roots. Then make a conscious effort to isolate those negative thoughts that drive your decisions and actions.

"Only by much searching and mining are gold and diamonds obtained, and man can find every truth connected with his being if he will dig deep into the mine of his soul."

—James Allen

Step 2: Control

Guard your mind. Once you have identified the dominant negative thoughts that hinder you from moving forward, use your willpower to take control of them. Never let them control your life and never make decisions or take action based on these negative thoughts.

Step 3: Alter

The most effective way to eliminate negative thoughts is to replace them with powerful positive ones. Feed your mind with motivating and empowering thoughts that support your goals and dreams. Put those new positive thoughts in writing. Divide a piece of paper into two columns. In the first column, write down every negative thought you discovered in the searching step. In the second column, write down the corresponding positive thought that you will use to replace the negative one.

Example:
Negative thought: I always fail.
Positive thought: I always learn new lessons.

"Let a man radically alter his thoughts, and he will be astonished at the rapid transformation it will effect in the material conditions of his life. Men imagine that thought can be kept a secret, but it cannot. It rapidly crystallizes into habit, and habit solidifies into circumstances."

—James Allen

Step 4: Trace

Monitor the effects of the new thoughts on your life. The positive results you'll see will encourage you to implement this 4-step process every time you discover a negative thought that you want and need to change. You can then replace your positive thoughts with even more powerful ones that will lead to better results.

Applying this process may not be easy at first, so keep in mind the three important characteristics that every smart farmer possesses and develops in order to reap a good harvest.

- **Patience:** Don't rush results. Changing negative thoughts that have been nurtured for years requires time. Be patient and work on one negative thought at a time.

- **Practice:** Like any new skill, mastering the 4-step process requires a lot of practice. But if you apply it to one negative thought after another, the process will eventually become second nature and you'll be able to implement it with ease and effectiveness.

- **Ceaseless Importunity:** This is the term James Allen brilliantly uses to describe what most of us call persistence. Never give up. Keep implementing this process until you weed out all the dominant negative thoughts that hinder your progress.

Changing your thoughts is the most powerful tactic you can use to change your reality and pave your way to a bright future. The effort you put into the process is worth mountains of gold and diamonds and the reward is a brand-new life full of abundance and prosperity. Search, control, alter, and trace with patience, practice, and persistence.

If you like mathematics, this next concept for replacing negative thoughts just might appeal to you.

Concept 2: Mathematical Insight on Positive Thinking

One of the earliest math lessons we all learn is addition and subtraction. We learned that the positive (+) sign increases the value of the output of the equation, while the negative (−) sign decreases the value of the output of the equation. So whatever number you add to a (+) sign guarantees you an output that is greater than the original number. And whatever number you add to a (–) sign guarantees you an output that is less than the original number. You can apply this mathematical fact to your daily life and make it work to help you become an extremely valuable and successful person.

The same concept of (+) and (–) signs applies to your attitude. When you are a positive person who tries to make the best out of any situation, then you will get greater results that are guaranteed to be better than the initial situation. The result you get doesn't depend on the initial situation you were in—it only depends on your positive attitude and how you responded to the initial situation, with the aim of increasing the value of the outcome. Conversely, when you have a negative attitude you transform any situation, whether it is good or bad to begin with, into a negative that is lower in value than the initial situation. Your negative attitude will decrease your value as a person, will not attract people to you, and will never get you good results.

Think about it. It is better for you to be a positive person who increases the outcome of whatever the circumstances are than to be a negative person who always complains, makes excuses, and transforms a situation into a negative outcome. Being positive is your only choice if you want to get better results. Being negative will add nothing to you or your life except more poor results that will lead to more failures. The (+) sign is much more powerful than the (–) sign. The key to better results and great success is having a positive attitude that can turn any situation into a positive outcome.

> *"A man's mind may be likened to a garden, which may be intelligently cultivated or allowed to run wild; but whether cultivated or neglected, it must, and will, bring forth."*
> —James Allen

Cultivate your mind into the most beautiful garden ever seen and let the beauty and light of your thoughts shape your actions and reflect on your life with abundance and happiness.

Virtue 3: Steadfastness of Purpose
Virtue 4: Evidence of Having a Mission in Life

As I was reading *The Alchemist*, a book by the fascinating storyteller Paulo Coelho, I came across a passage that truly inspired me and opened my eyes to a common life trap that most of us fall into. I told myself that this trap must be the ultimate drama of life. Here is the passage:

> *Everyone, when they are young, knows what their destiny is. At that point in their lives, everything is clear and everything is possible. They aren't afraid to dream, and to yearn for everything they would like to see happen to them in their lives. But, as time passes, a mysterious force begins to convince them that it will be impossible for them to realize their destiny.*

That is absolutely true.

Remember when you were young and used to daydream about your future? You had great hopes and aspirations, and you believed that the world was full of abundance and prosperity. You were motivated and had great trust in yourself and your ability to achieve your dreams. And suddenly, as beautifully stated by Coelho, a mysterious force began to convince you that it would be impossible for you to realize your destiny.

Now think about where you are in your adult life. Do the everyday hardships of life tend to distract you from your dreams? Do you spend most of your time just trying to survive and to fulfill your basic needs now that you're growing older and your responsibilities are increasing? Do you pay too much attention to what other people say and to their judgment of you? And finally, do you stick to your comfort zone and settle for living a mediocre life? That's the essence of the life trap that can lead to the above behaviors and more. It really is a mysterious force—but one that you can overcome.

The most important thing to understand is that greatness lies in your ability to bring your dreams back to life. Your greatness begins when you rediscover your true purpose in life. Your greatness begins when you realize what you love to do the most, what you do the best, and what contribution you can make to the world. Your greatness begins when you know who you truly are. Your greatness begins when you resolve to express yourself and unleash your potential to the fullest.

Whatever mysterious force affected you in the past, enough is enough. Today is your day. Breathe the fire of passion into all that you do. From today onwards, take complete control of your life. Decide, once and for all, to be the master of your destiny.

Today is the first day of the rest of your life. The past has passed. Focus on the present and strive for the success of your future.

Virtue 5: Identity with Spiritual Life

Modern life focuses so much on materialism that most people overlook the importance of feeding their souls and being in harmony with the universe. You are made of body, mind, and soul, and the spiritual component is essential for a balanced life.

During the difficult moments in our lives we naturally tend to focus on the spiritual realm. We feel that we are weak and so we seek the guidance and power of God. We pray and ask him for support and blessings. But the problem is that once our problems are resolved we forget that we need him every single moment of our lives. We think once again that we are in control and can handle whatever comes our way. So if you sometimes feel that something is missing in your life, that you are dissatisfied for no apparent reason, it simply means that your soul is being deprived of what nurtures and feeds it.

Personally speaking, God is the source of security and guidance for everything I do. By following his order and being connected to him every moment of my life, I feel secure that he will protect me from harm and provide me with the support I need to move forward and pursue my goals.

Develop spiritual practices like praying or meditating. Feed your soul and get connected with God. Feel the security, guidance, and balance you get from taking care of the spiritual part of your life, for it is *vital*.

Virtue 6: Evidence of Prudence

It is true that being wise is a blessing, but have you ever asked yourself what is the true meaning of wisdom? If you're like me, I always pictured a wise man as a very old man with white hair and a long white beard, a pensive man of few words who offered profound, thought-provoking advice after great deliberation. And I always thought of wisdom itself as ancient, little-known knowledge to be found only in fragile volumes of yellowed parchment. But is that truly what wisdom is? I asked myself that question for quite a while until I finally figured out what I believe is the true answer.

After interviewing more than one hundred successful people from all over the world—listening to and recording their success stories and timeless success secrets—I came to believe that every successful person is wise, and he who achieves massive success holds in his mind the true essence of wisdom. Therefore, to find true wisdom, you have to study their lives very closely and search for the clues they've left behind. What I discovered to be the true meaning of wisdom is summed up brilliantly by George Bernard Shaw: "We are made wise not by the recollection of our past, but by the responsibility for our future."

Being responsible for your life and your future gives you the wisdom you need to fulfill your mission in life. Having a clear vision of your future gives you an unparalleled advantage when it comes to successful decision-making and achieving better results faster. The truth is that *you* are responsible. This sense of responsibility is probably the foremost trait of ultra-successful people—they take responsibility for their futures, and that gives them the power to reach unmatched levels of success. You have to realize this fact now: no one can change your life but you.

People often tell me that they want a better life, but when I ask them what their vision of a better life is, they can't answer. Or they simply list some vague, wishy-washy things like more money or better health. You must have a crystal-clear vision and purpose because wandering aimlessly through life will not do you any good.

Your purpose and vision are the real sources of wisdom and power. Your purpose is the driving force that fires your motivation, gives you a sense of meaning, and holds you up to your dreams. The true meaning of wisdom lies in taking responsibility for your future and having a clear purpose in your life. As Stephen Covey says, "Whatever is at the center of our life will be the source of our security, guidance, wisdom, and power."

To be a truly wise man you need to do three vital things:

1. Take responsibility for your own future because no one else can be held responsible for improving your life. It is yours and nothing will change unless you take the lead.

2. Develop a clear vision of your future. Eliminate vague wishes and develop specific goals. Exactly how much money do you need? What kind of "better job" are you looking for? How do you define "better health"? Be crystal clear. Remember, you can't manifest what you can't see.

3. Take action. Be bold and create your destiny with your own hand. You might listen to thousands of tapes and read all the books in the world, but nothing will change until you take action.

Wisdom is the ability to see your future clearly and to craft a legacy that will make you live forever in the hearts and memories of others. Wisdom is the ability to make a difference and bring value to the world to make it a better place. Wisdom is the ability to live with purpose, know who you truly are, and mine your own diamonds.

Virtue 7: Freedom from Resentment

Here I want to touch on a very essential virtue for our emotional well-being. It is the ultimate power of *forgiveness*.

In today's world, amidst the cut-throat competition and the unhealthy race to excel, forgiveness is the only virtue that binds us together with our fellow humans and helps us retain our peace of mind. Most of us seldom think before we act, and we end up causing a lot of resentment among our near and dear ones. By forgiving one another for our misdeeds we drive out all the bitterness from our minds and save our relationships. In fact, the best gift that parents can give to their kids is to exemplify the importance of forgiving one another. Many researchers and medical practitioners also attach a lot of importance to forgiveness in the treatment of patients suffering mental distress. As Alexander Pope said: "To err is human; to forgive, divine." One who asks for forgiveness finds himself closer to God; one who bestows forgiveness experiences the divine joy of the act.

Forgiveness may be interpreted differently by different people. To some it may mean simply forgetting and starting fresh. For others it may mean learning from the experience and moving on. But the epitome of forgiveness on this earth is best exemplified by the kind of forgiveness bestowed by a mother to her child. Even if the child breaks all her rules, or all her crockery and precious crystal, or even her heart, she will always forgive him and stay by his side. This selflessness and unconditional love is the highest form of forgiveness. You may have a hundred reasons to hold a grudge against someone, but if there is one single reason to forgive, then simply forgive. It is also best to forgive someone right from the outset as doing so will relieve a lot of unnecessary stress.

> *"Forgiveness is freeing up and putting to better use the energy once consumed by holding grudges, harboring resentments, and nursing unhealed wounds. It is rediscovering the strengths we always had and relocating our limitless capacity to understand and accept other people and ourselves."*
> —Sidney and Suzanne Simon

In the movie *Home Alone*, we see that the elderly grandfather has been living alone for ages, away from his son and his family, simply because he is afraid that his son may not forgive him for some past transgression. His groundless fears had deprived him of years of precious time together with his only son and grandchild, time that could never be made up. And yet when he finally asks for forgiveness, his son welcomes him with open arms. This simple example demonstrates the power of forgiveness to set you free from the anger and hurt that you have suffered. When forgiveness is delayed or even denied, it most often results in a waste of time and peace of mind, which ultimately causes grave damage to our lives.

It's important to remember that forgiveness is an individual decision—a gift we give to ourselves, not to the wrongdoer. We forgive to free ourselves of hurt, not to somehow ensure that the offender will emerge a better person. Any form of injustice done against a person, if not forgiven soon, acts like poison. Once this poison spreads in your system it can impair you both physically and emotionally for years to come. Forgiveness is simply a way to extract the poison from our minds which could otherwise destroy our emotional state of well being.

On the other hand, if we are the offender and have hurt someone else by our words or deeds, it is equally important to forgive ourselves. This is more difficult than forgiving someone else; if not done, however, the effects are equally detrimental to our lives.

Forgiveness and Sacrifice

The word forgiveness itself signifies "to give up, to grant, or to give completely." Sacrifice means "to give up something you value in order to help others." To a certain extent, forgiveness and sacrifice go hand in hand. When someone wrongs us gravely, our innermost instincts as humans shout out for revenge. When we forgive, we sacrifice that primary desire to avenge ourselves on our offender. The result is definitely more beneficial in the long run, for us and all those concerned.

The level of sacrifice we experience depends on the gravity of the injustice done against us. For a minor altercation, our need for revenge is weak and so we do not really sacrifice much. If we have been caused great pain and distress, however, we would need to make a much greater sacrifice because our instincts would be clamoring for revenge.

Because of this element of sacrifice, forgiveness requires a great deal of strength and conviction. Think of the wife who discovers that her husband has been unfaithful. Think of the unimaginable distress and pain she must face. It would take a lot of sacrifice on her part to forgive him; she would have to compromise her own self-respect and even her love and faith in order to go on living with her husband. Even the person who receives forgiveness makes sacrifices; in this case, the cheating husband will sacrifice his self-esteem and the respect he once enjoyed within his family.

Forgiving is not always easy, especially when the misconduct has been very grave. It may take a lot of time before you can come to terms with it. However, you have to constantly remind yourself that the misdeed is a thing of the past and you have to get over it. How can you be at peace with yourself if you are constantly fighting with your past? Forgiving is the only way to ensure that all the bitterness of your past does not encroach upon your future. And whether that forgiveness entails sacrifice or not, it is definitely beneficial for both the giver and the receiver.

The Need to Forgive

Guy Finley, bestselling author of *The Secret of Letting Go*, had these thoughts on forgiveness: "In this life we are unable to forget whatever remains unforgiving. So, if we won't let go of some pain whose time has now past, then who is to blame for the weight of this burden still being carried on your back?" We need to forgive because it is the only way to get all the injustice done to us out of our systems once and for all. If we don't forgive, we will continue reliving the trauma which was inflicted on us sometime in the past. We need to forgive in order to snatch the power away from the offender to hurt us again and again.

Forgiveness brings along with it an unbelievable mental peace and stability, which was destroyed by holding onto resentment and indignation. Holding grudges can be deadlier than we think because it causes so much mental stress, trauma, pain, and even thoughts of vengeance. Such a disturbed state of mind could gradually damage physical well-being and cause ailments such as high blood pressure, diabetes, and even obesity and heart disease. One cannot enjoy life when the mind is full of bitterness. When a trauma is recreated every day, it most often becomes blown out of proportion as is the hatred toward the offender.

The best part about forgiving is being able to live normally as if nothing had happened. Forgiving does not mean forgetting the wrongdoing or inviting such conduct in the future. It simply means that you have decided to overlook something which you perceived as unjust and that you have learned from the experience.

Obviously, people who care for one another should avoid situations in which one needs to ask for forgiveness. However, the reality is that these situations do arise—so the most important thing is to forgive one another and move on together. Nurture grudges only if you want to kill your relationships and yourself as well.

Forgiveness is a difficult process but the choice is entirely ours. We can either hold on to our grudges and hurt ourselves afresh each and every day, or decide to forgive and let go of the pain.

Top 7 Benefits of Forgiveness

As we have discussed, forgiveness is the only way to recover from the pain caused to us by someone else's insensitivity, anger, or even betrayal. It is the only option for us to restore normalcy and freedom back into our lives and our relationships. The benefits of forgiveness are numerous.

1. Forgiveness is the best way to ensure that our hearts and minds function with lower heart rates and reduced levels of stress, which is the primary cause of all ailments.

2. We can reclaim our peace of mind and a good night's sleep without nightmares, both of which are vital for sound health. Forgiveness gets rid of all our negative thoughts and energies and replaces them with positivity.

3. Forgiveness fosters a healthy life, healthy relationships, and great self-esteem.

4. Forgiveness does away with all our depression, resentment, and vulnerability. It even keeps our self-sabotaging tendencies at bay.

5. All of our body's metabolic activities progress smoothly so we can enjoy great health of both mind and body.

6. Forgiveness brings us closer to God because he has commanded us to forgive one another. The joy experienced through forgiveness is truly unparalleled.

7. If you genuinely love yourself and value your life, then you deserve to forgive. Holding grudges and resentment against one another is a criminal waste of time and energy. It is easier to forgive.

By waging a war against someone else you can never expect to be at peace by yourself. The benefits of forgiveness are truly countless. So experience it for yourself and give forgiveness a chance.

<u>Top 7 Obstacles to Forgiveness</u>

Forgiveness is a process of the mind and it can only be developed through our conscious efforts and commitment. Convincing ourselves to let go of our hatred and pain requires a lot of strength. There are a few obstacles which normally block our path of forgiveness. They are:

1. **The will to forgive**. Most often we are highly obsessed with our need for revenge and our anger against our offender. We lack the will to forgive the one who inflicts pain on us.

2. **Violent emotions**. Whenever we are subjected to some grave misdeed, we retaliate by being emotionally violent. Our sense of extreme hatred or pain stops us from following the path of forgiveness. Sometimes the offender is overridden with an extreme sense of guilt. He may consider his act unworthy of forgiveness, which could also block the process.

3. **Self-pity**. A mind that is filled with self-pity and that is used to receiving sympathy from others would seldom opt to forgive. Forgiving and moving on in life would take all the sympathy away.

4. **Self-respect**. Sometimes, especially if the offense is really grave, our self-respect or even our ego will prevent us from forgiving.

5. **Lack of commitment**. Sometimes we may want to forgive but find it very difficult to be totally committed to the process of forgiveness. The same could hold true for the one who receives forgiveness.

6. **Grudges**. Whenever someone wrongs us, we nurture grudges against him or her. The more we think about those offenses, the

more they grow. When they grow out of proportion, it becomes almost impossible to forgive.

7. **Friends and family**. Our near and dear ones may also stand in the way of our forgiveness. We always seek counsel from the ones around us, and if they provide the wrong advice and we follow them blindly, forgiveness does not happen.

Overcoming the Obstacles to Forgiveness

There are different ways to deal with each of the seven obstacles.

1. **The will to forgive**. You have to tell yourself that you are suffering the consequences of someone else's action. By holding onto the pain, you are letting the offender hurt you all over again. How can you let anyone exercise so much of power over you so as to hurt you every day, even without being present? Believe in the virtue of forgiveness. Convince yourself that you deserve to be free from all this pain and opt for forgiveness.

2. **Violent emotions**. Whenever we are overwhelmed with emotions, we lose our sense of judgment. Meditation, yoga, swimming, and other forms of exercise are excellent means of getting a hold on our emotions. Be gentle on yourself. Once you have taken control of your emotions, you will be able to follow the path to forgiveness. Seek professional help if required.

3. **Self-pity**. Whenever we are victimized we most often like to bask in the attention and sympathy from the people around us. Stand in front of a mirror and look yourself in the eye. Shout out loud, saying, "I am the best and I can!" Keep shouting at yourself until you start believing what you are saying. You could also try helping someone else who has been victimized in the same way as you. By helping him or her overcome the situation you will feel your self-esteem coming back to you.

4. **Self-respect.** Sometimes we feel that by forgiving someone for his misdeed we are stooping too low and thereby losing our self-respect. But consider that forgiveness is for your own freedom. Anything that is in your own interest could never hurt your self-respect.

5. **Lack of commitment.** Put yourself in the shoes of your offender and try to visualize why he hurt you. You could also help out people in distress and help them forgive. Believe that forgiveness will make you a stronger and better person. Once you are committed to forgive, do not waver.

6. **Grudges.** Empathize with your wrongdoer. Think about the situation that led him to offend you. Be generous with him because you, too, must have been in his shoes at some point in time. Grudges will only chain you down. Shun them and choose your way to freedom.

7. **Friends and family.** Sometimes our friends and family give us biased opinions that prevent us from thinking liberally. Seek unbiased professional counseling to help you forgive.

Whatever the obstacle, do not let it stop you from forgiving and attaining freedom from resentments.

Virtue 8: Confidence in the Power of the Master as Teacher

It has been proven time and again that almost all successful people had a mentor. Most of them have been mentored by someone who is specialized and has achieved a high level of success in their same field. Having a mentor helped those successful people cut their learning curve into shreds and allowed them to leverage the experiences and knowledge of their mentors. You, too, must look for a mentor. Why go down a long path of trial and error when you can work with a mentor who has already traveled that path and can help you reach your peak performance level with lightning speed?

The best mentoring method is to work one-on-one with the expert in person. But there are other types of mentoring, too. You can read books, listen to tapes, watch videos, or attend seminars of the best people in your field. Then apply every idea they share with you to your own goals. Having a mentor is an important component to accelerating your success. It just doesn't make sense to reinvent the wheel. Other successful people have done it, and all you need to do is to find the best mentor out there and let him coach you and show you how to achieve massive success.

Go out now and search for your first mentor. Set a goal and then look for the best mentor to help you reach that goal on the fastest path possible. Successful people leave a trail of clues, and wise is the man who picks up those clues and leverages them to his best advantage.

Virtue 9: Confidence in One's Own Ability to Learn

Are you caught in a constant struggle for success? If so, I was once like you—and like so many other people—trapped in a situation where I thought there was nothing more I could do to reach higher levels of success. I read everything I could get my hands on and applied most of what I'd learned, but nothing seemed to work out like I ultimately wanted it to. But just when I was about to lose hope, a new horizon appeared before me. I discovered new lessons, ideas, and strategies that would take me to the next level.

When I think about my early start in business, I just have to laugh. When I compare what I do now with what I was doing before, I can only shake my head at the primitive level I was at. And what makes me laugh even more is that, at the time, I thought I was using the best techniques and strategies, that I was following the most advanced level of principles for business success—but the truth is that I was just applying the very basics.

So I'd like to share with you one of those universal laws of life. It's summed up in a wonderful proverb that says: "When a student is ready, the teacher will appear."

No one can learn everything all at once, or reach the peak level of success all at once. Life is a series of lessons and tests. When you learn a lesson and then pass the test that proves you've learned the lesson, you'll be ready to receive more advanced lessons. Life and success happen one step at a time. You can't take shortcuts. And if, by chance or by luck, you do take a shortcut, sooner or later you will return to your initial position—because along the way you missed some important lessons you need to keep you at your new level.

So even when you think you know it all, you must go the extra mile and keep on learning and searching for those new lessons. And you can be sure that when the time is right, the teacher you need—whether it be in the form of a mentor, a seminar you attend, or a book you read—will appear to teach you the next lesson that will take you to a higher level. But first you must be ready.

When you understand that learning must be continuous, you will not rush results or look for shortcuts. You will be patient and advance in life one step at a time, taking your time to learn and grow. Be sincere and have passion for your goals. Keep on learning and growing. Be committed and strive for success, because the quality of your commitment will determine the quality of the teacher who will next appear to you.

Virtue 10: Preparedness for Initiation

Imagine that you have an unexpected meeting with success. What would you do? Now, you might ask, "What do you mean by a meeting with success? Is this a new fiction story?" But the better question might be, "How can I have a meeting with success?" You might also be thinking, "I'm working very hard, reading everything I can find about success, and doing everything I can to achieve it, but nothing is working. I'm still struggling, still just hitting my head against the wall."

Well, I know what you mean. I can't count the number of times I tried to achieve success and failed. You probably agree with me that working hard is not enough anymore, right? Then let me share with you what history has proven to be the only guaranteed way to meet with success.

But wait—there's a catch here: you can only set up an *unexpected* meeting. Yes, I know it sounds odd, but that's the way it works. And I can only guarantee that you will have this unexpected meeting if you prepare for it in advance and make sure you're ready for it when it comes. If you are, then your life will never be the same. Every success story in history has followed the same path; I have seen this firsthand through my own personal experience and through the interviews I've conducted with successful people. If you still need more proof, just read the biographies of successful people and you will realize the truth of what I am saying.

Now, let me show you the magic.

Once upon a time, the great American poet and philosopher Henry David Thoreau offered this brilliant pearl of wisdom that enlightened the world: "If one advances confidently in the direction of one's dreams, and endeavors to live the life which one has imagined, one will meet with a success unexpected in common hours."

I don't know what I can add to such a profound bit of wisdom—it truly leaves this success guru speechless! You must have a dream and take action to achieve that dream. And when you least expect it, you will meet with success. Do your homework. Don't be like so many others who complain and place blame and try to lay the responsibility for their unfulfilled lives on other people and external circumstances. What do you want? What is the true purpose of your life? What is your dream?

If you already know, then you're more than halfway there. Now you must ask yourself if you are moving toward your dream. If you are, then congratulations—you have probably already met with success. And if you are not, never fear—you are sure to meet it very soon. If you do not yet know the answers to those questions, however, then you are the one who is blocking your own success. I know that may be hard to hear, but we must all face the truth.

Listen, it doesn't matter how many times you've set challenging goals but were unable to achieve them. The only thing that you need to do from now on is to make sure that every action you take advances your position in the direction of your dreams and toward living the life you've always imagined.

And you must advance *confidently*. Believe in yourself and your dreams. Believe that you have chosen the best way to live your life. That is the only path that will lead to success and ultimate satisfaction. I want you to read Thoreau's quote again: "If one advances confidently in the direction of one's dreams, and endeavors to live the life which one has imagined, one will meet with a success unexpected in common hours."

So here is the guaranteed formula to meet with success:

Confident advancement + Direction of your dreams = Meeting with success

I can't stress enough the importance of knowing your true purpose in life and knowing that your dream is worth living for. Moving toward a purpose and a dream that fires your desire and passion is the only direction that guarantees meeting with success. It all starts with confident advancement and your big dream, and voilà—the next thing you know you're meeting with success and experiencing a total life transformation.

Take action today and every day in one and only one direction: the direction of your dreams and your true purpose in life. Do this and be confident that you will achieve success sooner or later, in *unexpected common hours*. You're living your life anyway—why not live it in preparation for your meeting with success?

I urge you to prepare now, because success is coming your way in the next section!

Section 2:
Finding Joy In Your Life

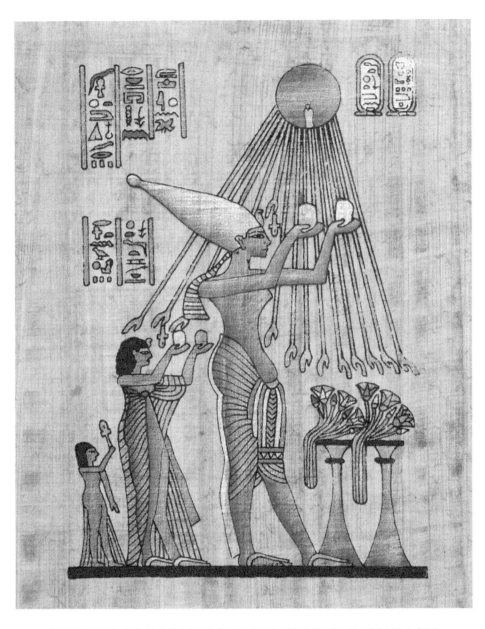

OLD EGYPTIAN PAPYRUS REPRESENTING PHARAOH
AKHENATEN MAKING AN OFFERING TO RA

Chapter 5
Your Life Begins Here

"If one tries to navigate unknown waters one runs the risk of shipwreck."

—Ancient Egyptian proverb written
on the Pharaohs' temples in Luxor

Napoleon Hill, author of *Think and Grow Rich*—one of the best-selling books of all time—and one of the earliest producers of the modern genre of personal success literature, once said: "To begin, you need to know what drives you. Simply because not knowing will mean that you can never begin to satisfy yourself. What does money mean to someone who hungers for love?" For me, these are the best words of wisdom I have ever read in my life. Therefore, I want to share with you this wisdom because it is the basic principle that puts you on the real path of greatness.

Let me ask you a question. Which of the following determines the direction of a ship in the sea: the direction of the breeze or the setup of the sail? In other words, if the ship is sailing toward a certain destination, what determines whether it gets there or not? Think a bit.

If you guessed the setup of the sail, then you are correct. The sail determines the direction of a ship in the sea because the direction of the breeze is variable and uncontrollable. But the captain of the ship has full control over the setup of the sail. Now, imagine that the captain of the ship doesn't know his destination and he is just sailing. In your opinion, how can he decide which is the best setup for the sail?

Surely he will never be able to make such a decision. He doesn't know where he wants to go so he will never have control over his direction at sea. Whichever direction the breeze blows is the direction he will go. Occasionally, our captain may face a strong storm, which can break down his ship. He will lose everything because he isn't able to correct the setup of his sail in order to face the storm. Maybe the breeze will take him to a place he doesn't want to go at all. You see, he has no control because he doesn't know his destination. He doesn't know his *purpose*.

Now I think you've started to get my point. The sea is your life and the captain is you. If you know your destination before setting sail, you will have full control. What is your purpose for the journey? What is the purpose of your life?

You must answer the above questions before taking a single step. When you find an answer, you will master your life. You will have the control. You will know which sail setup will take you to your destination. The external circumstances may be very tough, but you will be able to face them in the proper way. You will be able to maneuver your ship and take different routes because you will know your direction very well.

The secret of joy, greatness, and power is to know exactly what your purpose in life is. Only then can you start the journey with full control of your sail against any breeze that comes up. Remember, *it's the set of the sail, not the direction of the breeze, that determines where you go in life.*

Two Universal Laws for Success

In this section, you're going to learn how to use two powerful universal laws to help you become the wealthiest, most successful man you've ever imagined. This may sound like hype, but you will discover that all successful people throughout history have used these two laws to attract massive success and craft their legacies. I am going to show you, with proof, that these two laws can help you succeed in whatever endeavor you choose.

Everyone is now talking about *The Secret*, a movie created by Rhonda Byrne that is taking the world by storm. The movie reveals an old universal "secret" that has been discovered and rediscovered by top success philosophers throughout history. All successful people agree that this single secret is behind every success a man can achieve. Sure, there may be some naysayers out there, but the truth remains: *The Secret* is the key to every success in the history of mankind.

Now I would like to share with you the first law that *The Secret* is all about, the greatest law of success of all time—the Law of Attraction. In simple terms, the Law of Attraction says that likes attract likes. The theory is based on the scientific fact that thoughts are made up of a vibrant energy that radiates out into the universe and attracts similar energy from the universe.

For example, if you keep thinking that you are poor, you will attract more scarcity and poverty into your life. If you think that the world is abundant and that opportunities are everywhere, you will attract more success and more opportunities. The energy that you radiate attracts similar energy. In other words, whatever energy you put out into the universe, whether negative or positive, will come back to you. Now imagine that you have a dream that dominates all your thoughts and you have the intention to achieve that dream. This dominant intention will act as a huge magnet that can attract all the resources and opportunities that can help you make your dream a living reality.

The advertising genius P.T. Barnum once wrote: "The great secret of success in anything is to get a hearing. Half the object is gained when the audience is assembled." And that brings us to the second universal law, which is a corollary to the Law of Attraction. It also happens to be the first law of marketing: Get Attention.

When you set the intention to achieve your dream, the Law of Attraction will immediately start working for you to attract the attention of "the likes" that match your goals and that can help you get what you want. But your intention must be really powerful. You must think of it from a marketing perspective, where your dream is the product and your intention to achieve that dream is the marketing effort you employ to make the product highly successful. If you can't captivate the media and get the "hearing" you need, then your dream cannot thrive. If you fail to assemble the audience, then your dream will die. That is why most people fail to get what they want—their intentions are too weak and lean more toward wishes and hopes instead of decisions and commitments. Their marketing efforts are also too weak and fail to attract the attention of the audience and the media that is needed to create a big buzz around the product.

Your dream must fire your soul. It must be so big that your mind becomes like a huge magnet that attracts any resource or opportunity that can help you. *The level of your desire and passion to get what you want is the determining factor of your success.* Set the intention to achieve your dream and make it so powerful that it can get the attention of the whole world. So powerful that it can bolster you against objections and criticism. So powerful that it helps you face the naysayers, take the risks, and be courageous.

> *If your desire is __not__ greater than your fear,*
> *you will fail.*

Now let's look at a surefire way to activate these two laws in your life and make them work for you on autopilot. You may be wondering how you can set the right intention and how you can make it so powerful that it will attract the attention of the world and detonate the ultimate power of the Law of Attraction. The answer is simple, something that every self-help book makes crystal clear, something that they all agree is the one thing that you must know to acquire wealth, happiness, and everything else you desire: *You must know what your life purpose is.*

Everyone, including you, is unique and was born for a certain purpose. You are equipped with gifts and talents that can help you fulfill that purpose. You have unique desires and passions for things in life that correspond with your true purpose. The strongest intention that you can set, the strongest energy that you can radiate, and the detail that can detonate the greatest power of the Law of Attraction is that intention which matches your true purpose in life. Your purpose in life is what the world is waiting for you to deliver because no one else on earth can fulfill that purpose. So when you find it and set the intention to live it, it will form a powerful, attention-grabbing force that will command the whole world to start working by your side. Opportunities will start to flow like magic simply because you have responded to your unique call. God created you for that purpose and when you respond to that call, God will make everything that can help you flow your way.

Your true purpose in life lies at the cross point of your talents, passions, and the world's needs. In other words, it is what you love the most, what you are best at, and what you can contribute to the most. To truly know these three core areas, you must dig deep within yourself. You must know yourself through and through. Your life purpose is the essence of who you really are. *Starting now, using these two laws, you will attract more success and abundance to your life.*

If you do not know your true purpose, you will never be able to radiate a powerful thought that resonates with the reason for your existence. You will never be able to attract the attention you need to help you respond to your call and fulfill the purpose that the whole world is waiting for. Following your true purpose in life puts you in harmony with the whole universe and opens the doors to unlimited wealth and abundance. You're ready for success and wealth, aren't you?

See yourself knowing exactly what you want, having a clear purpose in life, and mastering the two greatest universal laws of success and wealth. And shortly, you will find opportunities flowing into your life like magic. You will be able to achieve success, wealth, and happiness in a way you could never have imagined possible.

WARNING: Are You Living Like a Busy Bee?

Albert Einstein once said: "A perfection of means, and a confusion of aims, seems to be our main problem." Look around you. Many people seem to be as busy as bees, working hard and striving to excel. There they are in their little hives, aspiring to succeed and seeking perfection in everything they do. They feel great joy when they receive praise from others for the quality of their work. But after a while, those busy bees stop to realize that despite all of their hard work, they just aren't collecting enough honey in their honey jars—that is, they are not moving forward or getting the results they desire.

Big problem! When people feel that their desired outcome is out of their reach no matter what they do, they simply lose hope. They start to put less effort into their goals and enter a downward spiral of negative productivity. Even worse, they are shocked when their fresh, brilliant coworkers get promoted—and they remain in the same hive, doing what they excel at, still receiving praise for their quality work but not winning the opportunity to move to a bigger, better hive.

I want your unconscious mind to listen very carefully to the wisdom of Einstein as he brilliantly states the root cause of this problem and provides a powerful solution. Read his words one more time: "A perfection of means, and a confusion of aims, seems to be our main problem." As you read on, you'll understand how you can end the disappointment and reap the rewards of your hard work.

The root cause of this hard struggle lies in being incorrectly focused on the means and on the perfection of the means. Are you too busy making a living that you lose track of the true purpose of your life? Do you focus on the work itself and lose sight of its meaning and purpose, the reason you're doing it in the first place? What is the purpose of your life? Why are you doing what you're doing? What is your aim?

Too often I receive e-mails from people who complain that they work really hard but never get the expected results. Then I ask them for their motives, their reason why. That's where I see a lot of confusion: those people have vague or unfocused aims. And that's where the problem lies. Before you start on any endeavor you must identify the reason—the purpose. You must be crystal clear on the *why*. Knowing the why will give you continuous focus, meaning, and motivation along the way. When you are clear on your purpose, you will find a way to achieve any goal and you'll be able to make better decisions about which path you should follow. You might even realize that the hard work you're doing will *not* lead to your desired purpose.

When you are clear on your main purpose, your mind will act like a huge magnet to attract the opportunities that will help you achieve your desired outcome. In essence, don't waste more time, energy, or money trying to only acquire knowledge and perfect your work, which are just the means to your desired outcome. Instead, take some well-deserved time to think through your goals and to delve into the big picture of your life. First, as we discussed earlier, start by searching for the reason for your existence. What is your true purpose in life? What are you passionate about? What contribution do you want to make to the world?

Then, on a smaller scale, define the reason for every action you take and analyze how it matches up with your true purpose. Will it take you closer to your aim or move you farther away from it? By doing so, you will create not just success, but *everlasting* success. If you define your aims, you'll start to experience a period of clarity, satisfaction, and joy. You'll increase your ability to find the correct and fastest means to achieve your desired outcome. The why activates your mind power to unimaginable levels so that when you focus on the why, the how will take care of itself. When you have a clear purpose, the problems just won't matter. And you'll be sure to fill up your honey jar beyond your wildest dreams!

The Power of Purpose vs. The Fear of Failure

If you are one of those people whose dreams seem to keep slipping out of your hands, you may be the cause of your own suffering. Let me explain by sharing with you the one single thing that makes any dream impossible to achieve and how you can overcome it.

When I was in my teens, I always tried taking different paths to my dreams. But every time someone told me that the path I'd chosen was too difficult, that it would be too hard to achieve what I wanted, I'd just quit and leave that path behind. I wasn't persistent at all. I was held hostage by the "dream killer." And I let it kill one dream after the other, until one day it no longer could. I'll tell you why it couldn't in just a few moments, but first I want to let you in on that one single thing that kept hindering me on the path to my goals.

That one single thing is the fear of failure. When you focus on failure, you will always end up quitting—and that is the biggest mistake you can make. Fear of failure has killed a lot of dreams, and will keep doing so for generations to come unless we raise the awareness that fear of failure is our closest friend. We just need to understand how to deal with it, and I have some key points that will help you to do so.

You have two ways to respond to your fears: you can let your fear of failure control your life and kill your dreams, or you can pursue your dreams anyway and know that at least you have a 50% chance of realizing them. If you choose the first path, you are 100% guaranteed not to achieve your dreams and to live a mediocre life until your last breath. If you choose that second path, then you have a 50% chance of living the most fulfilling life you can live and to unleash your full potential. And let me tell you this—if you are persistent, you will have a 100% chance of achieving your dreams no matter how many times you fail along the way. As long as you are still in the game you have a chance to win. But why did I tell you that fear of failure is your best friend? Let's go back to the part of my story where fear of failure could no longer stop me from pursuing my dreams.

The day fear of failure lost its power over me was the day I discovered my true purpose in life. The power that my purpose gave me was so much stronger than any fear could ever be. I no longer listened to people who told me that I would fail. I no longer listened to my own negative thoughts. And I no longer let myself be stopped by self-limiting beliefs. When you discover your true purpose in life, a tremendous power will flow through your veins. You will become truly unstoppable.

When that moment came for me, I gave thanks to the fear of failure. And you will too, because the fear of failure can lead you to discover your true purpose. When fear can no longer stop you from pursuing what you want, then you will know for sure that you have found the place where your greatness lies. Fear of failure is the number one dream killer only for those who don't know how to deal with it—but it can be your best friend if you understand that your fear is really a great clue that can guide you to your true purpose.

Don't ever let the fear of failure stop you. The best way to overcome it is to follow a path where your desire to achieve a goal is much greater than the sum of your fears—and to persist, persist, persist.

Now that you are armed against the number one dream killer, you're probably ready for success, right? Then read on, because in the next chapter I'll show you my proven 7-step system to finding your true purpose in life.

Chapter 6
7 Steps to Finding Your True Purpose in Life

"Is he who walks prone upon his face better guided,
or he who walks upright upon a right path?"
—Quran: Surah Al Mulk: 22

Victor Frankl, an Austrian neurologist and psychiatrist as well as a Holocaust survivor, once said: "Ever more people today have the means to live, but no meaning to live for." The biggest problem is that we base our choices in life on what is expected from us rather than on what is meaningful to us. Take a look at the following questions and answer them honestly:

- Are you dissatisfied at work and uncertain about your future?
- Are you having difficulty with your life?
- Are you experiencing a lot of hard times?
- Have you faced a lot of crises?
- Does the "busyness" of life make you lose clarity?
- Are you searching for a meaning to your life and work?
- Are you just focusing on setting goals without knowing where those goals will take you?
- Are you looking for work that aligns with your talents and passion?

If you answer yes to any of those questions, then the only way out is to discover your *life purpose*.

Every life has a natural reason for being. Trees have a natural reason for being. Animals have a natural reason for being. And that means that *you have a natural reason for being*. That also means that your life is incomplete until you discover your purpose, your passion, your uniqueness, and your *value*. The good news is that your purpose is already within you, just waiting to be discovered. But the busyness of life and the rush to make a living and be secure might have made you forget why you are here and what you want to do with your life. Purpose gives you a sense of direction. It helps you make the right decisions at the right time. It helps you live your true values. It helps you express yourself and be who you really are. Purpose allows you to live a life of ultimate satisfaction. Purpose is the way to unleash your full potential. A purpose-centered life gives you a reason to wake up in the morning and an overall sense of meaning. A meaning for your work. A meaning for your time. A meaning for your pain. A meaning for your pleasure. And a meaning for *yourself*.

> *Your heart needs a passion. Your soul needs a meaning. Your mind needs a focus. Your life needs a purpose.*

Cancer therapists Carl and Stephanie Simonton give their patients this advice: "You must stop and assess your priorities and values. You must be willing to be yourself, not what people want you to be because you think that is the only way you can receive love. You can no longer be dishonest. You are now at a point where, *if you truly want to live, you have to be who you are.*"

When I discovered my life purpose, everything in my life changed. I felt that a tremendous amount of power was coming out of me. Now I can face hard times, tough people, and difficult situations that I would never have been capable of handling before. That is because I discovered my core where my true power exists—and this power is unstoppable. And the burning desire attached to that core can burn away the largest obstacles you could ever imagine.

The Life Purpose Discovery System

The moment I discovered my purpose is the moment when I decided to develop the Life Purpose Discovery System. It's easy to follow and can help you discover the true meaning for your life and understand what type of "giant" lies within you. Get ready for the most valuable hours you will ever live in your life. Get ready to awaken the giant within you. Get ready for the life you have always dreamed of. Get ready to fulfill the burning desire that fires up your soul.

Let's begin…

Overview of the Life Purpose Discovery System
Step 1: Discover the WHY

The system begins with the most important and most universal question: Why? Why do you need a life purpose? You will never be able to discover your true life purpose without having a strong reason that urges you to find it. The reason for your search may be that you are suffering from a meaningless life that causes you too much pain. Or perhaps you feel an intense desire for self-fulfillment and satisfaction, which can only be gained through fulfilling the purpose that is ready to explode from within you.

Life purpose discovery is not just a "nice" skill to learn, nor is it an optional element to be used in the pursuit of a better life. The need for a life purpose must be deeply embedded in the core of your soul. You must feel that having a purpose is as essential to your well-being as your body's need for food and water. My friend, believe me or not, you can't live a true and meaningful life without having a clear purpose that ignites your core desires.

The next three steps take you through the Logical Discovery process. Here you will use your mind to logically set in order the facts that cover your basic understanding of yourself and your life. You will use this logic to identify your passions and talents as they relate to the world's needs.

Step 2: Find Your Passion

In this step, you will analyze your past to assess those moments that were the greatest, the happiest, and the most pleasurable. You will identify those activities that make you lose all sense of time while you're doing them, the activities that you would like to spend your whole life doing—even if you receive no money in return.

Example: I am passionate about success and human potential.

Step 3: Identify Your Talents

Once you find your passion, you will then identify your talents, the things that you do better than anyone else. Your talents are God's gift to you and they make you unique and special.

Example: I have the ability to motivate, inspire, and empower people.

Step 4: Determine Your Contribution

In Step 4 you will answer the question, "What value can I add to the world?" The true calling and purpose of your life lies in the cross-connection between your passions, talents, and the world's needs.

Example: I can help people transform their lives from making a living to making a difference.

Once you complete the Logical Discovery, you will have the common ground and the basic information from which you can extract and write the first draft of your life purpose statement. Then you will move on to the Emotional Discovery process where you'll begin to evaluate your draft statement. You will use your emotions to clarify your work up to this point so that you can be absolutely certain that the purpose you identified is truly right for you.

Step 5: Define the Level of Your Desire

In this step you will answer the question, "Do I have 100% desire to live for that purpose?" The purpose of this step is to unleash the power of intense desire and ignite a fire that never goes out.

Step 6: The Power of Solitude

The Emotional Discovery process will require moments of solitude—extended periods of time in which you will meditate and reflect on the desire in your soul. It is at this point that you will strive to find the connection between your true self and this life purpose. Sitting alone in peaceful surroundings, with only nature for company, is a wonderful way to open the gate to your inner guide, the guide that will lead you in the right direction.

Step 7: Future Projection

Finally, you will use a Future Projection technique to create a lens through which you can "see" yourself living this purpose and the effect it will have on your emotions in the future. Will you feel completely satisfied and fulfilled by living that life?

Once you've completed the Emotional Discovery process, you will be ready to write the final version of your life purpose.

The Life Purpose Discovery System is a powerful tool. The tremendous results of applying this system are beyond imagination and can help you define your purpose and ultimate value to the world.

Now, let's get into the details and start going through the system step by step.

Step 1: Discover the WHY

"Motivation is the fuel necessary to keep the human engine running."

—Zig Ziglar

Jim Rohn, the world's leading motivational speaker and business philosopher, once said: "When you know what you want, and you want it bad enough, you will find a way to get it." Since you are reading this book, I assume that you have enough reasons for having a life purpose. Because without a burning desire for a meaningful life, without a strong foundational core, and without the right setup for the sail of your life, you cannot reach true achievement and satisfaction. I am going to start you off with a process for discovering the compelling reasons for having a life purpose. As much as I may try to convince you and tell you what you will gain by discovering your life purpose or what you will lose by not discovering it, you need the conviction of the truth of all this to ultimately come from deep inside of you.

So let's begin the practice.

Focus on your current life. Focus on the *now* and do the following:

Answer the question "What would happen if I discovered my life purpose right now?" by writing down five changes that would occur in your current life. These should be things that would give you immediate pleasure.

1. ---
2. ---
3. ---
4. ---
5. ---

Write down five things that are causing you a lot of pain because you don't have a purpose for your life.

1. ---
2. ---
3. ---
4. ---
5. ---

Now focus on the _future_, twenty-five years from now.

What pleasures will you have because you discovered your life purpose twenty-five years ago? Write down five things.

1. ---
2. ---
3. ---
4. ---
5. ---

What pains are you suffering from because you _didn't_ discover your life purpose twenty-five years ago? Write down five things.

1. ---
2. ---

3. --
4. --
5. --

From the _now_ section, choose the two most compelling reasons—one that would bring you extreme pleasure and one that is causing you extreme pain.

1. --
2. --

Next, choose the two most compelling reasons from the _future_ section—one that will bring you extreme pleasure and one that will cause you extreme pain.

1. --
2. --

Pleasure and Pain Drivers

The two extreme pleasures I will gain from having a life purpose:

1. --
2. --

The two extreme pains I will suffer due to not having a life purpose:

1. --
2. --

Take a moment to really feel these pleasure and pain drivers. Don't move on to the next step until you are totally eager for the pleasure that is waiting for you after discovering your life purpose, and totally suffering from the pain of not having a life purpose. Remember, you can do anything if you have a strong reason why. Now that you've discovered your compelling reasons for having a life purpose, let's go to the next step, the Logical Discovery.

The Logical Discovery

In this part of the system you will start using logic and facts to set the basic foundation and collect the necessary information to discover your life purpose. This process contains three basic cornerstones: passion(s), talents, and world needs. These three cornerstones set the interconnectivity between your true self and the outside world.

What you love most represents your passion. It is based on the principle that says that you only excel when you do something that you love. What you do best and what represents your uniqueness are your talents. Your talents are the gifts you were given to use in fulfilling your reason of existence. The value you can add to serve the world and help others to live a better life represents the world needs. Your life purpose lies in the cross connection between you and the world.

"You are your own scriptwriter and the play is never finished, no matter what your age or position in life."
—Denis Waitley

Step 2: Find Your Passion

My friend, have you forgotten your passion? Do you live without spirit? Do you miss love in your life? Do you miss motivation? Do you feel that you are living a life that is not consistent with who you are? Do you feel that you are drifting far from your dreams? Let me ask you: Where is your passion? Where is your heart? Remember the best and most unforgettable moments of your life and search for your passion. Look for what you love to do and that which you hope you will never stop doing.

Look for the desire to do this thing even if there is no return in money or fame or any other kind of reward. You do "it" just because you love doing "it." Stand up now and search for your passion. Shout out loudly, "My passion, come to me!" Living with passion is the essence of excellence and the core of satisfaction.

Did you know that you can instantly know whether you will be successful or not? All of us want to be successful, but there is a big difference between what we want and what we have. So let me give you the clue to know whether what you are currently doing in your life will lead you to a successful future or not. You will no longer be moving around without confidence as to what your future will be. You will know, without any doubt, whether you are on the right track or whether you are moving toward a disappointing future.

Here is the secret revealed by Michael Korda, bestselling author and publishing executive: "Your chances of success are directly proportional to the degree of pleasure you derive from what you do." That's right—no real success can be achieved without loving what you do and you will not have enough motivation to persist with goals without loving what you do. If you hate what you are doing now, whatever it is, then you have very little chance of success.

You may be thinking, "What can I do? I am in a college that I hate, but I must finish" or "I have a job that I can't leave because I have too many responsibilities, especially financial ones." Those questions may hold your current truth and I cannot tell you to quit what you are doing because it will not lead you to success. But what I can tell you is that you must be on a path where you love what you do. And to do that you have to start *now* to define your life purpose, you must complete the process that you've just started.

Defining your life purpose is the first step toward a satisfactory and successful life. You have to know the path that will let you live with passion and make a difference in other people's lives. When you discover your life purpose, you will have the power to make little changes, one at a time, until you are aligned in the right direction—the direction of your life purpose and your ultimate destiny.

You will not change your path overnight, but you can start now under your current situation by doing the necessary preparation and by making very small changes, changes that will build up over time. These changes, along with another and then another, will soon have you on the right track. Here is the secret again: "Your chances of success are directly proportional to the degree of pleasure you derive from what you do." Past is past. Search for your life purpose now in order to survive your future and live with passion.

To help you discover your passion, answer the following questions:

1. What subjects do you most enjoy reading about?

    ----

2. What television or radio programs do you most enjoy?

    ----

3. What are your favorite types of movies?

    ----

4. What are your favorite hobbies or pastimes?

    ----

5. What subjects do you enjoy discussing with friends?

    ----

6. What have been your favorite jobs?

    ----

7. If you doodle, what do you often draw?

    ----

8. What are your favorite toys?

    ----

9. In which moments and situations have you felt the greatest satisfaction, fulfillment, or sense of comfort with yourself and the world around you?

----

10. What great dream would you dare to dream if you knew it was guaranteed to come true?

----

11. If your doctor told you that you had only six months to live, how would you spend the rest of your time?

----

12. What kinds of activities or situations bring you the greatest joy?

Now list the top three things that you are extremely passionate about.

1. --
2. --
3. --

Once you identify your passions, move immediately to your birth gifts—your talents.

Step 3: Identify Your Talents

Everyone is special in something and if you focus on developing your specialty and uniqueness, you will become a person of ultimate value and you will achieve unlimited success. God gave you special talents solely to fulfill the reason of your existence. These talents will help you achieve your life purpose. There is a life principle that says that energy flows in the path of least resistance—and the path of least resistance is the path of your talents, the things that you can do with the highest quality and least effort. Talents come in all forms, so look in every corner of yourself to find them. They may be as simple as reading fast, innate creativity, a sense of humor, and curiosity, to more complex talents like researching, assembly, problem solving, teaching, parenting, motivating others, working with teams, persuasion, writing, logical thinking, programming, drawing, and so much more. Your talents and passions are your ticket to excellence.

To help you discover your talents, answer the following questions:

1. What are the abilities that come naturally to you and are inherent in your personality?

    ----

2. What talents, abilities, or character traits would you like to develop further at this point in your life?

    ----

3. What tasks have brought you the most success?

    ----

4. What tasks do you think you could do well, but you haven't yet done?

    ----

5. If I had a magic wand and could grant you one skill or ability, what would you choose?

List the top three areas in which you are most talented.

1. ---
2. ---
3. ---

Once you've defined your talents, move immediately to your contribution.

Step 4: Determine Your Contribution

What is your description of an ideal world? What matters concern you the most now? What do you want for the people of the world? What difference would you like to see in the world? What do you feel that you can do to make that difference? When we talk about "the world's needs," we must remember that the term can encompass everything from the needs of your family to the needs of the whole world. Historical figures, world leaders, and transformational individuals have a passion for serving the whole world. Figures like Gandhi, Newton, and Einstein are examples of those whose lives changed the world. Many other successful people are very happy and living an extraordinary life, but they use their passion to serve their little communities or just their families. It doesn't matter whether you go big or small—what matters is that in the end you use your talents and passion(s) to serve.

For example, you may bring up a child to be a future world leader. Although you focus on just one person, you add great value to the world by preparing one of tomorrow's leaders who can transform *our* lives. You must add value to the lives of others. My own principle in life is that *success is about service*.

To help you discover the world's needs in your opinion, answer the following questions:

1. What type of volunteer activities do you prefer?

   ----

2. If you had to give three messages to the people of the world, what would they be?

----

3. If you won a million bucks, what would you do with it?

----

4. If you ran the world, what changes would you make?

----

5. If you were assigned a single task that would change our lives for the better, what would you like this task to be?

----

6. In your opinion, what are the three major aspects of an ideal world?

----

7. What three major changes would you like to see in the world before you die?

----

8. Who are your role models in life, the people you admire most? What areas do they serve?

----

9. What legacy do you want to leave? How do you want to be remembered?

List the top three needs that you feel the world is waiting for you to fulfill.

1. --

2. --

3. --

By now you have set the facts, collected the information, and gone deeply inside and outside yourself. Now do the following:

- List the top passion from your list of three.

- List the top talent from your list of three.

- List the top contribution from your list of three.

These are what I call the Triple Core.

Finding the interconnection between the Triple Core is the secret of discovering your true purpose in life. Now that you are armed with the Triple Core, you can write your first life purpose statement. Get ready, your life is about to begin!

Your Life Purpose Draft Statement

The secret of discovering your life purpose lies in the ability to find the cross-connection between your passion and talents and the world's needs/your contribution. Sit quietly and think about how these three cores interrelate. Where is the cross connection? Take your time and think deeply. Don't rush it out until you are ready to write one statement that represents the interconnection between the Triple Core.

If you find it difficult, use this magic formula to structure your sentence:

Talents > Passion > World's Needs = Life Purpose Statement

Start by writing your top talent. Then state how you are going to use this talent to satisfy and live your passion. Finally, state how you are going to use your passion and talent to satisfy a world need.

Example of a life purpose statement:
Talent: creativity
Passion: movies
World need: inspiration for success

Statement: My life purpose is to use my creativity to create movies that will inspire others to live a successful life.

Another example:
Talent: writing
Passion: reading novels
World need: enriched soul

Statement: My life purpose is to write novels that enrich people's souls.

Now start writing yours. You can use the above formula or you can construct your own statement. The most important thing is that you must write a short statement that you truly believe in.

My Life Purpose Is:

Once you've completed the Logical Discovery, you are ready to go through the most important part of the system where you will evaluate the above statement on the emotional level.

The Emotional Discovery

"Let others lead small lives, but not you.
Let others argue over small things, but not you.
Let others cry over small hurts, but not you.
Let others leave their future in someone else's hands, but not you."

—Jim Rohn

The purpose of the Emotional Discovery process is to put the first draft of your life purpose statement under emotional evaluation. Emotional energy is the fuel that will take you toward whatever destination you choose. Since we are talking about a *lifelong* journey, you will need to have enough fuel for that journey, which means that you must have a sufficient emotional reservoir. The process begins with knowing the level of your desire for the purpose you defined in the Logical Discovery. You will examine your 100% commitment and "heart attachment" for that purpose.

Then you will start opening the channels between you and your inner guidance and intuition. You will start listening to the voice of your soul and the essence of your calling. You must be able to sit alone in complete solitude. Solitude is the gateway to your inner guidance where you will find the true answer for whatever you are searching for, which in this case is your life purpose.

The final part of the Emotional Discovery process is the "future projection." In this part you will start imagining and living, in your mind's eye, your desired future. You will feel the emotional reflection on that style of living. You will write a complete life scenario in which you portray your life after twenty-five years of living your purpose. You will draw the details of a future reached by living that purpose.

Once you've completed the Emotional Discovery section, you will have the well-rounded, unstoppable motivation and persistence to live and fulfill your life purpose. You will start the true life that is emerging from the most important part of yourself—your heart. Of course you know that your heart plays a vital role in your physical life, but it must also play a vital role in your personal and spiritual lives. You must play your unique heart's symphony. If you don't live from your heart, you may function on the physical level, but you'll be dead on the emotional level.

Life must be lived with passion. You only have one life, so you must live it as you want and in your own way. Be who you are. Live your dream. Live with passion. Unleash the power within you. Live the true you. Live your purpose. Live your legacy.

Step 5: Define the Level of Your Desire

Your life purpose needs intense desire and persistence to sustain itself. While fulfilling your purpose, you will face unexpected failures and obstacles. You will meet people who are dream vampires and dream robbers. You may reach a point where you feel that there is no way out, a point where you are totally disappointed. You may face massive and destructive failure. You may face enemies who wage war against you. To be able to face all that you absolutely must have 100% desire, which will in turn lead to consistent persistence.

The fire of that desire must have the ability to burn and melt any obstacles, situations, or people that stand between you and your purpose. That burning desire gives you the power to stand up again, regardless of how many times you have fallen. Are you willing to live and achieve the purpose you have discovered, regardless of what you may face, risks you may take, sacrifices you may need to make, and pain you may suffer? Are you ready to trade short-term joy for long-term success and satisfaction? Do you have the intense desire to live your purpose? Do you really want it?

> *Desire is the fuel of success.*

On a scale from 1 to 10, where does your desire to fulfill your purpose stand? If your desire doesn't score a 10, then you can do one of the following:

1. Ask yourself: What will it take to make my desire a 10?
2. Repeat the first four steps of the Life Purpose Discovery System.

Hint: "Without a sense of urgency, desire loses its value." —Jim Rohn

Step 6: The Power of Solitude

Since you are discovering your core, you need to dig deep inside, get to know yourself better, and identify exactly what you want. Relaxing, listening to meditative music, and having long, quiet times with yourself are very helpful practices that open the channels for you to know and understand the only person about whom you have the least knowledge—*you.*

I highly recommend that you experience this time of solitude out in nature, because in nature the gateways to creativity and meditation are wide open. In periods of solitude, reflect on your current life and search for what is really missing. Ask yourself, "Is this purpose what I really want?" To live from the inside out you must know yourself very well. You must know who you truly are, what moves you, and what your passion is.

Before you go to sleep and when you wake up in the morning, ask yourself again, "What is my purpose in life? Is this purpose what I really want?" It is very probable that if this purpose is truly yours, you may even cry. Yes, you may cry. It will touch you deeply and make you feel that you are born again. Let me ask you this: What is the first thing you did when you came into this life? Yes, you cried!

After this period of solitude, you should have a clear picture of what you really want and have a sense of emotional attachment (or detachment) to the purpose that you stated for your life.

"Take time to be quiet."

—Zig Ziglar

Step 7: Future Projection

Travel with your mind twenty-five years into the future. See yourself there living your purpose. How can you describe this life? Do you like it? Do you feel passionate about it? Do you have an intense desire to live this life? Will you be satisfied by what you have done through living this life? This part of the process is extremely important because you may feel very enthusiastic about what you have discovered up to now, but afterwards you may lose this enthusiasm.

Twenty-five years from now, how is the spiritual part of your life? How is the personal part of your life? How is the social part of your life? How is the physical part of your life? Who are you? What are you doing? What things do you have?

With this vision of your future in mind, write a one-page scenario on the following issues:

Main themes of your life twenty-five years from now.

Major expected pleasures (in terms of success, achievement, and satisfaction).

Major expected pains (in terms of obstacles, challenges, and failures).

Major expected risks and sacrifices.

Then ask yourself, "Am I willing to live this life for the sake of living and fulfilling my life purpose? Do I still have 100% desire?" If not, then start the system from the beginning. In fact, if at any point during the system you find yourself less than 100% convinced, enthusiastic, and motivated to live your stated purpose, then stop and start from the beginning.

The major reason for not succeeding with this system, for not being comfortable with the purpose you have stated, or for feeling that the journey may not be that easy, is that your *why*—the reason you need to have a life purpose—is too weak. The good news is that if you feel you must begin the system from the top, this time you will have much more knowledge about yourself than before—which will only give you better clarity about the purpose of your life.

If you have passed this final step, then congratulations! You did an excellent job!

Now write your final life purpose statement:

My Life Purpose

Now Your Life Begins!

Before we move into the next topics, I just want to tell you something between you and me. I was like you, without a purpose. I will not say that I lived a hard life or faced a lot of difficulties in terms of money or education. I was, however, a very ordinary person. Sure, I was living a very good life in terms of things like a good family, a good education, good friends. It seemed as if everything was available to me. But you know what? I wasn't satisfied.

I was searching for my soul, searching for a meaning, searching for my true potential. It took me six years of searching to finally find myself and my life purpose. That day, my friend, was the most important day of my life. Everything changed dramatically from that point on. I felt that I was born again, but this time I was born to win. I felt a tremendous power filling me. And you, too, will feel these things when you find *your real purpose*. You will experience a very strange sensation inside you. You will feel a true power within. You may cry. You may laugh. You may shout out loud. You will feel it. Only your feeling will tell you the truth about your life purpose.

Trust your feeling.

When I discovered my purpose, my life changed completely. I did things I was never capable of doing before. I started building the life that I always dreamed of. Now I live with passion. I wake up every day with full enthusiasm to move closer toward achieving my dreams. When I experienced that change, I decided to dedicate my life to helping you and others to discover the power of a *purpose-based life*.

You don't need six years to discover your life purpose. By applying the Life Purpose Discovery System, you can discover your life purpose in one year, one month, one week, or even one day. It depends entirely on you and how deeply you are connected with and know about yourself.

My friend, don't let this chance slip through your fingers. Do it now! Reading alone will not accomplish anything for you. It is only the beginning. Apply what you have learned so far. Answer every question and go through each step and always finish a step completely before going to the next one. This is your life and it's worth living. It's worth living good. It's worth living *great*! Yes, I know that you are living now, but you deserve to live a real life, a life with *passion*.

Finding your life purpose will transform your life until you are living on a world-class level. You will be amazed at yourself and the power that you will find inside of you. I am sure of it because I lived this moment myself— and I really want you to live it, too. Yes, you can. You are great. You deserve success. Believe in yourself. Search for your soul. Live on purpose. Live the dream. Be who you are. Unleash your giant. Fulfill your destiny. Craft an ultimate legacy. My friend, the world needs you.

Now your life begins.

Chapter 7
The Critical Factor

"Peace is the fruit of activity, not of sleep."
—Ancient Egyptian proverb written
on the Pharaohs' temples in Luxor

You'll never make a difference in your life or in the world if you discover your purpose but then sit still doing nothing. The critical factor in achieving anything you want in life is *taking action*. Action is the catalyst of transforming your dreams into reality. Nothing will change unless you act. Growth and prosperity are directly connected to taking bold actions and avoiding procrastination. The path to peace and achievement is paved with action, not with sleep.

Here are three keys to kick starting your journey toward a purposeful life.

Key #1: Momentum

The pharaoh Khufu built the Great Pyramid of Giza, the only remaining wonder of the seven wonders of the ancient world. It contains an estimated 2.3 million blocks of stone weighing on average about 2.5 tons and constructed over a twenty-year period. The Great Pyramid was the tallest man-made structure in the world for over 3,800 years. Nothing has ever been built that comes anywhere close to rivaling its technical prowess. Many engineers agree that we could not even build it today, in the 21st century.

This majestic structure was simply built one stone at a time. Any major achievement is completed one task at a time. Nothing worthy is done overnight. In fact, what people see as overnight success in another person might have taken that person ten or twenty years to reach. What you need to do is to just *start*—and then keep the ball rolling. The most important gear in a car is first gear, which gets the car moving from a stationary position. Then as you move faster, you can see that the gears and fuel use decrease. Once you gain enough momentum to get you moving fast, less energy is required to keep you moving. But getting the car started is the most difficult stage of all. Therefore, you need to employ different tactics to get yourself started.

One of the best tactics that I use is to decide on the easiest and most effortless action that I can take that relates to a certain goal. What is the single smallest, easiest action you can take? Once you discover what that action is and then act on it, you will get into the process and find yourself gaining momentum to take you to the next action. Did you ever sit down to read just a few pages of a book and then find yourself finishing a few chapters? That is the power of momentum.

The need for perfection might be your biggest enemy. Many people keep procrastinating because they are waiting for the perfect time and the perfect circumstances to take their first action. They feel that if all the stars are not aligned perfectly, that if they can't complete an action perfectly the first time, then they might as well not even begin. You must know that nothing can be done perfectly the first time, that everything needs to be improved over time. Give yourself permission to improve, because nothing is perfect. Overcome this myth of perfection and just take action and improve daily. Again, the key is to gain momentum, to shift gears and use less energy to get you moving at faster rates.

The power of momentum can also be used to develop new habits or stop bad ones. When you want to develop a new habit, start with one small, extremely easy action and then build on that. You can do fifty-two pushups after one year if you just do one more push up every week. If you want to stop smoking, just stop smoking one cigarette a week. Over time you will find yourself quitting smoking. Learn to break down big tasks and work on very small segments, one at a time. That's the best way to acquire *momentum*.

Remember that if you procrastinate because you're waiting for the perfect moment to develop or stop a habit, that moment will never come—unless you face a disaster like a heart attack, and who wants to wait for that?

Some people see the path to their goal stretched before them and think that it is just too long and daunting. Let's look at the example of a student. Perhaps this student wants an MBA but sees a three-year path in front of him. He thinks, no, that is simply too long for me right now, I'll just wait for the perfect time to begin. What I want to ask that student is: "Aren't you going to live those three years anyway? Which do you prefer—that after these three years you have an MBA or you find yourself in the exact same position as you are now?"

On the other hand, some people undervalue the significance of small tasks. They feel that they are irrelevant. After all, what would one pushup more a week really do for me? It's nothing, a trifle. If you're one of those people, then you must learn the power of accumulation.

The Power of Accumulation

Small things accumulate to form long-term success. This is something successful people know and how success stories are built—step by step. Think about all the little everyday things you do that result in long-term achievements. Reading ten pages every day will result in finishing a 300-page book in a month and twelve books in a year. Writing a third of a page every day will result in writing a 360-page book in three years. And who knows? You could become a bestselling author. Can you imagine the amount of fame and credibility you'd receive just by completing those little things?

The primary reason behind all great success stories is the concept of continuous improvement. Commit yourself to the continuous improvement of all areas of your life—physical, mental, and spiritual. Do little things every day to improve your relation with God and create peace in your life. Improve the personal area. Improve your career. Do an excellent job even on small tasks. Improve your finances. Save, invest, and give something to charity. Improve the social area. Spend some time with your family, friends, and spouse. Participate in charity work. Improve the physical area. Exercise, eat healthy food, drink water, and breathe fresh air. My friend, small things really do make a difference. Continuous improvement is the key to long-term success. Improve every day and your future will take care of itself.

Just remember, all you need to do to make great advances is to *gain momentum*. You will require less energy as you move forward and you'll find yourself achieving significant goals faster and more easily. It's all about getting started—just find a way to begin and let the power of momentum and accumulation play in your favor.

Key #2: Productivity

The scribes were the intellectuals of Ancient Egypt. They occupied the upper rungs of the social ladder and enjoyed recognition and respect accordingly.

The scribes were meticulous record keepers who wrote down every possible transaction. The precision with which they calculated quantities is impressive even by today's standards. Scribes had to be good mathematicians and their calculations of the labor and materials needed for major construction and building projects display a considerable degree of algebraic skill.

Scribes also worked for the government, recording numerous statistics about food production, harvests, and taxes for analysis and planning. Government officials were usually scribes who had worked their way up into higher government positions. By giving senior officials an overview of the country's total stocks, the scribes helped make possible their orderly distribution, the creation of reserves, and the planning for special projects.

Other documents from the scribe's pen included regulations issued by various governmental bodies, court proceedings, and records of private contracts dealing with sale and purchase, loans, hire, financial arrangements between spouses, inheritance, receipts, taxes, accounts, and so forth.

So what is the lesson here? The secret of productivity and effectiveness is to know your numbers! Studying your statistics is an important element for improving your results in life and business.

Most people walk through life without properly analyzing how they spend their time, money, and energy. That would be fine if they kept quiet and accepted their positions in life. But instead they complain that there just isn't enough time to accomplish everything they want. Or they complain of not having enough money to buy the things they desire. Or they claim that they have limited energy and get exhausted quickly, and as a result they can't spend leisure time with their family or friends.

Although you may have limited resources of time, money, and energy, you can still use them in the best way possible to achieve what is most important to you in your life. What you might be missing is the awareness of your daily habits and behaviors that would help you determine how you currently spend these resources. If you start calculating and keeping records of how you spend your time, money, and energy, you will be shocked by the huge amount of those resources being wasted on activities that are not important at all. Statistics are not as complex as you might think. In this context, I use the word simply to mean keeping records and monitoring the trends of your daily activities to see how you spend your most valuable resources.

Practically speaking, I strongly advise you to keep logs of all your resources. The first should be a time log. For a period of one week, record every single activity you do. It might be difficult at the beginning, but keep it up. Come on, it's just one week of commitment—and as a result you will experience a dramatic improvement in your productivity and effectiveness. You'll learn a lot about yourself and your behavior. You'll know where your hours go, when they are wasted, and when they are well spent. Once you have this awareness, it will be possible to allocate and plan your time to perform your most important activities and focus more time on your goals. You'll know exactly how to take control of your time and how to save it for your desired outcomes.

For your personal finances, keep a log of your income and expenses for one month. Record every monetary transaction and, at the end of the month, study the results. You will be surprised. I am sure you'll find some expenses and credit card usage that weren't necessary at all. You'll have a better view on how to use your money more effectively. You'll have more control over your finances and will be able to save money for what you really want and need. This awareness of where your money goes and where it comes from is essential for better money management and wealth creation. Warren Buffett says that the very first rule of investing is "don't lose money."

For your energy, keep a one-week log of your energy levels. This concept might be new to you, so let me explain. Every day, keep a log of the hours in which you were fully alert and active and those in which you were lazy or tired. Draw two lines on a sheet of paper, one vertical and one horizontal.

On the horizontal axis, write the hours of the day from the moment you wake up in the morning until you go to sleep at night. On the vertical axis, write the numbers from 0 to 10. These numbers represent your energy level, with 10 meaning fully active and 0 meaning fully exhausted. Now, for every hour on the horizontal axis (which represents the current hour in your day), put a mark next to the number from 0 to 10 that represents your energy level for that hour. At the end of the day, draw a curve by connecting the points you marked. This curve will show you your energy levels throughout the day. Repeat this process every day so that you can recognize the pattern of your average energy curve. This way you will know your general active hours and lazy hours.

You may ask, "What is the purpose of knowing my energy level curve?" Simply by scheduling your most important tasks of the day—those that need a lot of effort and concentration—during your most active hours, you will become ultra-productive. Save the easy or unimportant tasks for the lazy hours when your energy and concentration are low. Do you see how this can make you ultra-productive? How often have you spent your most active moments doing routine or easy tasks, essentially wasting those productive hours on activities that require minimum effort and concentration? And then, when the time comes to do heavy tasks, you find yourself exhausted. That's when you start to procrastinate and perform low-quality work.

Do you see how statistics can be turned into massive success?

These examples can be applied to business as well, especially the money log. You should monitor your profits, income, and expenses. You should study your accounting figures and your balance sheets. I have a story for you that will illustrate how knowing your numbers and recording your statistics can result in a profit boost without acquiring more customers or selling more products.

I have a friend who works in stationery distribution. Every year he used to purchase a huge stock of stationery and keep it in his inventory. His yearly profits were low, but he settled for them because at least his business was profitable. One day he decided to hire an accounting firm to record his finances and cash flow and provide a report of his financial position at the end of the year—and that's when he got quite a shock. The accounting firm confirmed that the year had been very profitable. "Oh, that's good!" my friend said. But wait—it wasn't that good. The accounting firm told my friend that he had an excess of money held hostage in the form of unused inventory. Almost 50% of his inventory stock was not used at all. So, for the next year, they advised him to buy only 50-60% of the amount of stock he used to buy every year. And guess what the result was? That's right—50% of his wasted money in unused inventory will go directly into his profits for the new year.

It's easy to see how knowing your numbers and recording your stats can result in dramatic improvements in your life and business. Starting today, keep logs of your time, money, and energy. The information you learn will allow you to have more control over the way you use your resources. You'll achieve better results and you'll experience a dramatic acceleration of success.

The pharaohs realized this secret thousands of years ago and they made sure to dedicate their most intellectual human resources to doing their record keeping and statistical analysis. Now it's time for you to follow the pharaohs' code to maximize your productivity and effectiveness and turn your statistics into massive success.

Key #3: Systems

Beginning with the reign of Snefru, the first pharaoh of Egypt's 4th Dynasty, entire towns were associated with each of Egypt's pyramids. These towns were full of people employed solely for the purpose of maintaining the king's afterlife. New villages and agricultural estates were founded specifically to supply the pyramid cults and those who worked for them.

To build and maintain the pyramids, an enormous support system must have existed. There would have been great need for facilities for production, building materials, pottery, supplies, and food, as well as storage depots and housing for the workmen and all those responsible for servicing the pyramid temples. In fact, evidence of sewage systems has been uncovered along with the oldest known paved street, complete with drainage facilities.

What is the lesson here?

When you have a big dream or goal, you need to create an equally big support system to help you achieve it. The purpose of any system in general is to create a set of well-defined actions that lead to *consistent* results 99% of the time. Of course, there will always be that 1% of special cases because no system is ideal.

There are two types of systems: operating systems and support systems. An operating system is comprised of a set of actions that lead to certain results that are directly related to the goal you want to achieve. It provides a way of structuring the day-to-day operations of every person and every activity involved in that goal. A support system takes care of the personal or operational needs and provides the optimal environment for you and all those who are working to achieve the goal.

For example, a sales system is a type of operating system that is directly related to the business goal of generating profits. A human resources system is a support system put in place to support the management and to provide employees with the basic needs necessary to help them perform at their best. If your major goal or dream is related to your career, then developing a system for your personal growth would be a type of operating system because investing in yourself is directly related to your goal. Having a loving family, on the other hand, is a kind of support system that provides you with love and support and creates the relaxing environment you need to help you move forward with your dream.

After this long introduction, you've probably begun to understand a big trap that most people and businesses fall into. Usually, the major focus is put on the operating system—and most people see support systems as a luxury. Big mistake! You can't build a skyscraper without a very strong foundation, so laying that foundation is the first step you need to accomplish before you attempt to execute the rest of the blueprint. Don't spend your time writing plans and taking action before you lay the foundation of success. For example, when employee performance decreases, the boss may put more management pressure on the staff to increase performance—but the core problem is that the employees are not getting the rewarding salary they need to satisfy their basic needs and those of their families. Management didn't provide them with a good support system and therefore their performance decreased.

On a personal level, when you focus solely on your career and ignore your family, you destroy one of the most important support systems in your life. You think that spending time with your family and nurturing your relationships with them is a waste of time, and that your time would be better spent pursuing your career goals. But as time goes by, you'll lose the security and comfort of a blessed home and you'll get steamed up by the stress and tension of your workaholic lifestyle. So don't ever overlook the importance of developing good support systems in both your life and your business.

The first support system that you must develop is the *Basic Needs System* that will provide you with food and shelter. No one can achieve a big dream if he is starving or shivering out in the cold! Once you establish a good support system that consistently provides you with your basic needs, then you can build on that and start developing the operating system that will put you on the first step toward your ultimate goal.

The second support system is the *Sewage System*, which works consistently to get rid of the waste in your life and business—all those activities that exhaust your time, effort, and money but don't lead to significant results. You can't imagine how dramatically you can improve your life and business if you simply get rid of those fruitless activities.

Another useful support system is the *Storage System*, which provides a way to store any kind of information or materials that you might need in your operating system. For example, you can create what I call the "ideas treasure box" to store powerful ideas that you think could dramatically improve your life and business if you implement them now or in the future. In this age of information overload, this is a brilliant support system for organizing your ideas and thoughts. Instead of forgetting ideas or falling into the trap of implementing dozens of them at the same time—which would stretch you to the limit—you can just write them down and store them in a file. Then, when the time is right, you can simply take out your ideas treasure box and pick one idea that you can implement now—just one at a time!—and see the immediate improvements it creates.

When I started The Success Avalanche (www.Success-Avalanche.com) project, one of my aims was to create an ideas treasure box for people just like you. I recorded interviews with over one hundred successful people that led to over sixty hours full of success stories, insight, and wisdom that you can use any time you need motivation or a new idea to take your life and business to the next level.

Yet another powerful support system is the *Paving System*—or the *Problem-Solving System*—which eliminates the obstacles and resolves the conflicts that hinder you from smoothly achieving your goals. One of the main steps or actions that you *must* include in your problem-solving (paving) system is *finding a solution*. The biggest mistake people make when it comes to problem solving is that they spend endless hours focusing on or defining the problem itself, which actually shouldn't take more than 10% of the time. Then 80% of your effort should focus on answering one important question: What is the solution? The remaining 10% should focus on answering the question: How can we prevent this problem from happening in the future?

As a leader you must remember that your number-one role is to build either an operating or support system, or even both. As Stephen Covey has said: "Management works *in* the system; leadership works *on* the system." Develop systems that even a fool can follow because the role of a system is to simplify, not to complicate. The role of a system is to provide clarity and well-defined actions that lead to consistent results 99% of the time. When you develop systems for your life or business, work first on the support systems—because without them, you will be subject to total breakdown and failure.

I shared with you some examples of powerful support systems for you to consider. Now I want you to think thoroughly about your specific situation in life and ask yourself, "What kind of support systems am I missing or can I develop to take my life or business to the next level?"

The pharaohs developed huge support systems to build the magnificent pyramids. Follow the pharaohs' code and develop even bigger support systems to build your magnificent dream—and to build your own legacy. And remember that "systems" mean consistency, simplicity, and clarity. Go systemize your way to success!

Momentum, productivity, and systems are three important "action" keys in your journey to fulfill your purpose in life—the journey that will take you to a place of maximum joy and satisfaction.

Next, we're going to discuss the five keys to maximum joy.

Chapter 8
5 Keys to Maximum Joy

"For every joy there is a price to be paid."
—Ancient Egyptian proverb written
on the Pharaohs' temples in Luxor

How are you living your life? Are you living it your family's way, your society's way, your friends' way—or your own way? Are you living an inherited life that has no taste or meaning for you? Are you giving other people full control of your life and your destiny? Do you try to please everyone but yourself?

All of us have been told at one point or another that our elders know more than we do and that we should follow their advice. Are you following the advice of people who don't know you and who don't know what your dreams are?

There Is Only One True Success

I know I am asking too many questions, so let me be frank and share with you the message I want to drive home:

> *"There is only one success: the ability to live your*
> *life in your own way."*
> —Christopher Morley, American writer and editor

That is the *one* true success! Read that quote again.

Your ability to live your life from the inside out is the only true success. Success comes in all shapes and sizes and is highly dependent on each individual's personal definition of what success means to him. But in the end, everything converges on this tipping point: any form of success *must* reflect your own way of living your life. You were born for a unique purpose, and the best way to live your life is to fully express that purpose. The ultimate victory in life is to win the battle over the external forces that push you to live your life like everyone else, to follow the herd like a sheep, and to deprive yourself of your right to live life in your own way.

There is only one way to unleash your inner giant and that is by being determined to live your life by your own rules and making the commitment to find your true purpose and turn it into a living reality. When you do that, you will reach your maximum personal power and will experience an overwhelming sense of meaning and satisfaction. Only then can you craft a legacy that will ensure that you live on in the hearts and minds of others for years to come.

Let Christopher Morley's quote be the guiding light in your life and the guiding principle in your quest for success. Search for what makes you feel *alive*, not for what makes you a living. Life is a gift from God and you must make the best use of it. Ask yourself, "What one action can I take *today* to start living life in my own way?"

The Real Trick to Living a True Life

Do you wake up every morning looking forward to living a beautiful and fulfilling day? Or do you feel bored and wake up to one meaningless day after another? I came across an amazing quote that contains one letter that makes all the difference. This one letter expresses the true essence of life and encompasses the wisdom of how to live a truly extraordinary life. Let me share with you this quote:

"The real trick is to stay alive as long as you live."
—Ann Landers

See the letter *A* in the word *alive*? That letter is the key. All of us are living our lives, but very few of us truly feel *alive*. Having passion for your life and doing what you love is the key to creating an extraordinary life. Aliveness is the feeling of living life to the fullest. It is waking up every morning full of energy and exhilaration. Aliveness is living your life with passion and enthusiasm. It is acting with a sense of meaning and purpose. Aliveness is having a sense of contribution and doing things that make a difference. It is crafting your legacy with every action you take. That is how you should live your life. That is how you deserve to live your life. You deserve to not only live, but to be alive.

You are meant for a great purpose. Find it and live it—and in that way, you will feel alive every moment of your life. The real trick to living a true life is to find what unleashes your potential and makes you feel alive. The real trick to living a true life is to stay alive as long as you live. From now on, don't waste a moment doing something that sucks your energy and turns you into a dull person. Find what makes you feel alive and do it every day. Stay alive as long as you live and you will make a difference and leave the world a better place to live in. Aliveness is the key to greatness. Do what you love and give it all you've got.

Now here are five keys to help you live your life to the fullest with maximum *joy*.

Key #1: Simplicity

Daily life in Ancient Egypt revolved around the Nile and the fertile land along its banks. The annual flooding enriched the soil and brought good harvests and wealth to the land. People generally built their own mud brick homes, grew their own produce, and traded in the villages for food and goods they could not produce themselves. Most ancient Egyptians worked the land as field hands and farmers, or worked as craftsmen and scribes. Only a small minority enjoyed the privileged lifestyle of the nobility.

Despite the majestic legacies left behind by the ancient Egyptians, you can see from this scene of their daily life how simply they lived and how important simplicity was in their lives. The fact is that simplicity is an important key to finding joy in life. You can always see and feel the simplicity in the ways of thinking and living of successful people. They understand that simplicity opens the doors to great opportunities and makes them more admirable and attractive to others. Successful people believe that simplicity gives them access to greatness. As Leo Tolstoy once said, "There is no greatness where there is not simplicity, goodness, and truth."

Our modern-day lives, however, tend to be very complicated, which makes our ways of living and thinking complicated as well. To truly be successful and experience the joy of life, you need to use your creativity to discover a way to bring your life back to simplicity and peace. Consider what Henry David Thoreau once said: "Simplicity, simplicity, simplicity! I say, let your affairs be as two or three, and not a hundred or a thousand. Instead of a million, count half a dozen, and keep your accounts on your thumbnail."

"Simplicity is making the journey of this life with just baggage enough."
—Charles Warner

So get rid of all those "extras" that do nothing but clutter up your life and keep you from attaining joy. Remember that the ancient Egyptians built their homes from mud bricks—and yet they still managed to build those marvelous pyramids! It is easy to discern the beautiful lesson left to us by the ancient Egyptians—that simplicity is the path to joy, peace of mind, and greatness. Try your hardest to protect your attitude from the complexities of modern life and work on developing simple ways of living—and of doing business as well.

Einstein's Code for Peace of Mind in Daily Life

Albert Einstein once said, "Everything that can be counted does not necessarily count; everything that counts cannot necessarily be counted." How much money do you have in your bank account? And when was the last time you spent some quality time with your family?

We tend to give too much importance to things we can count, like money and houses and cars. But tell me honestly, when was the last time you went to sleep with complete peace of mind and a contented feeling of gratitude? In our daily lives, we often overlook the things that really count simply because we can't measure them. We fight for position, money, and power and forget about the greater purpose of our existence. We forget that we are here to contribute to and make a difference in the world.

Why must you focus on the things that matter? Simply because that is the only path to happiness and satisfaction. Yes, money is good and being rich is a true blessing. But remember that money never brings true happiness and satisfaction—the way you *use* the money does. Therefore, you must not overlook the small things that connect your body, mind, and soul and hold the real essence of life. If your money is not put into service, then it is a wasted value.

Think about this: nothing can compare to a moment of total gratitude and inner peace. Nothing can compare to those special seconds when you feel that you're in complete harmony with the universe. The true joy in life is hidden in the things you can't measure—a baby's smile, the beauty of nature, breathing in pure, fresh air. Those things are what represent the true value of life. Focusing on collecting money and material goods is a very exhausting endeavor. You can be the richest man in the world but when you're on your death bed, you'll find that the little things you overlooked in your life are what matter to you most. Your value, your legacy, and what you have contributed to the world are the only things that will ensure you pass out of this life with a big smile on your face.

Starting today, pay more attention to the things that can't be counted. End each day by reflecting on what you are most grateful for in that day. Live every moment with a peaceful mind and a loving heart. Think simply, live simply, and do business simply. That is one of the big secrets to finding joy in your life.

Key #2: Family

The ancient Egyptians had large families with an average of four to seven children. Boys were expected to help their fathers and girls their mothers, and all children would usually stay in the family home until the ages of thirteen to fifteen. At that time, they would be expected to get married. Although some marriages were arranged, people more often married for love. There was no formal or legal marriage ceremony—people simply set up a common home together as a declaration of their union. A woman would usually be given a dowry, which would remain her property throughout the marriage or in the event of divorce.

The ancient Egyptians clearly valued family life. And it surely must be valued by anyone who seeks joy in life. The love of a family is one of life's greatest blessings—and the family is the only place where you can find unconditional love. As George Bernard Shaw once said: "A happy family is but an earlier heaven."

Now, mark the word *happy*. Don't ever fall into the trap of ignoring your family for the sake of your career, fame, or fortune. One day your family will be the only people standing beside you in your last moments of life. They are the strongest support system you will ever have. The time devoted to your family is time very well spent.

Nowadays, people tend to put less importance on building a happy family. Or even if they do understand its importance, they still claim that they don't have time to spend with the family. Why? Because they are just too busy working to provide their family with money and security.

Be honest with yourself. If you lose your family, all the success in the world would have no meaning. You may not realize that now, but rest assured that at a certain point in time this truth will become crystal clear. As Winston Churchill said: "There is no doubt that it is around the family and the home that all the greatest virtues, the most dominating virtues of human society, are created, strengthened, and maintained."

The impact of your family on you and your life is unmatched. Yes, there are some special cases in which the family becomes a nightmare. If that is your situation, then you must work to build a virtual family of friends, relatives, or whoever it is you feel closest to. The bottom line is that you need the emotions that come with having a family. And no matter what mistakes your parents made while bringing you up, you must believe that they were trying to do their best. They never meant to harm you.

Let me share with you a brilliant way to build a happy family. The idea is illustrated perfectly in a proverb that says: "Treat your family like friends and your friends like family." Need I say more? Building a happy family is worth every effort you put into it. Remember—family comes first. That is what the Pharaohs realized thousands of years ago.

Key #3: Balance

The Egyptians were the first people to fish for pure pleasure. Nobles are often shown in armchairs, lazily dangling lines into their well-stocked garden pools. During the Old Kingdom, fish were usually netted or speared, although angling did become popular later. Fish could be roasted or boiled, salted and preserved, or dried in the sun.

Over time, wild animals such as the lion, the bull, and the cobra came to represent royalty. The power and danger seen within the lion and the wild bull became synonymous with the pharaoh. From pre-dynastic times, images of the bull trampling the enemies of the king represented the pharaoh's triumph over his enemies. The bull implied strength and power, while the lion was a representation of the pharaoh's power and leadership, and was often hunted by the pharaoh in a symbolic show of courage.

Having fun is an essential part of a balanced life. And a balanced life is essential for your general well-being.

The three centers of balance relate to your three components as a human being, which are your body, mind, and soul. You must feed your mind and grow as a person in terms of skills and in terms of career progress. Also, you must take care of your body and physical health as we will examine in the next key. Finally, you should consider the emotional and spiritual parts of your life.

As Stephen Covey says, you need time to sharpen the saw—a time to regenerate your vitality and enthusiasm. You need time off from everything you do, including the pursuit of your dreams. In addition to developing good relationships with family and friends and saving some time just for them, it is also essential to have time just for yourself.

Think about how you spend your leisure time. What are your hobbies? Having a hobby is an important aspect of the balance equation. A hobby reflects your personality and attracts like-minded people. Spending time engaged in a pleasurable hobby feeds your mind and soul. Personally, I really like chess. My heart dances when I see the chess board. Of course, chess is not my purpose in life, but I feel very happy and satisfied by spending hours in front of the chess board playing against a friend. It just satisfies me and helps me take time off just for me and for the sake of pleasure. You might like hunting, playing music, reading, writing, or whatever. The most important thing is that you develop a hobby that keeps you in balance and helps you renew yourself and your enthusiasm.

Balance is a natural law. Everything tends toward balance. If your life is out of balance or if you focus on only one aspect, like your career, for example, you will find a great deal of suffering in other areas of your life. If that happens, take it as a warning that your life is out of balance and that you must act to fulfill your other needs as a human being.

Think about all the interesting hobbies you enjoyed in your childhood that are now totally neglected or forgotten in the hustle and bustle of your adult life. Perhaps you occasionally express with a regretful smile how much you loved the time spent pursuing those hobbies. There is no need to look back with regret! Now is the time to rediscover those former joys and give yourself permission to immerse yourself in your lovely hobbies and enjoy a little "me time."

Balance your life. Set aside time for your body, your mind, and your soul. Doing so will make you feel complete and your joy will increase. Balance is one of the essential laws of the universe and we *must* respect it.

Key #4: Health

Ancient Egyptian medicine was a mixture of magical and religious spells, with diagnoses and remedies usually based upon a keen observation of the patient.

As many illnesses and conditions were regarded as the result of either malevolent influences or erroneous behavior, the most common procedure for dealing with many problems was to use an amulet or magical spell. Once the practitioner had dispersed or neutralized any malignant influences or evil spirits, he could then usually begin to treat the patient medically, if required.

In the modern world, it is well known that the two major pillars of good health are nutrition and exercise. However, I'm not going to talk a lot about them in this context. Instead I want to focus on a new perspective, which is how to be healthy from the inside out.

Have you ever seen a woman in her nineties with the fresh, bright face of a twenty-year-old girl? Conversely, have you ever seen a young man in his thirties with the dull, ruined face of a ninety-year-old man? That's right— being healthy isn't just about age and diet. There is an entirely different way to be healthy and stay young. But how can it happen?

As James Allen has said: "The body is the servant of the mind." Those are eye-opening words of wisdom. Your thoughts create your habits—so negative thoughts create negative habits, which in turn lead to a sick, weak body. Even if you follow a rigorous regimen of diet and exercise, you'll never be healthy if you let your mind be controlled by anxiety, fear, envy, and depression.

Positive thoughts, on the other hand, create positive habits, which in turn lead to a strong body and a healthy mind that are ready to tackle any obstacle in your path. So the bottom line is that if you want a perfect body, then work from the inside out. Guard your mind and fill it with healthy, positive thoughts.

"Out of a clean heart comes a clean life and a clean body."
—James Allen

The most powerful tactic to develop a well-guarded mind is to live with passion. Doing what you love and what truly makes you come alive will make your heart flourish and fill your life with happiness, satisfaction, and purity. Injecting passion into all that you do will help you live every day with an evergreen body full of energy and enthusiasm. Illness will have a hard time finding its way to you—and even if it does, you'll recover quickly simply because your heart, soul, and mind are passionately attached to your dream.

The smart farmer knows intuitively that the quality of his harvest depends mainly on the quality of his seeds and his soil. With all its power and capabilities, modern technology will never be able to generate a good harvest from spoiled seeds planted in bad soil. Feed and nurture your mind with positive thoughts, for it is the guaranteed way to living a healthy life—and indeed may be the perfect recipe for health that no one is telling you about.

Of course diet and exercise are also important, for to enjoy life and live it to the fullest you must take very good care of your body. After all, you body is the host of your mind and soul. It is your companion in your life journey. If you don't take care of it, you stand to lose a great deal. You might feel powerful now in your youth and taking care of your body might not seem so relevant. But you may regret that idea later! Being healthy should be on the top of your priority list, because how on earth are you going to achieve great goals with a sick body?

So although you need to pay attention to diet and exercise, remember that they are secondary to a healthy mind. Don't reverse the process—work from the inside out, or you'll never get the results you want. James Allen has said that there is no physician like cheerful thought. Heed that brilliant advice and you'll be on your way to living a healthy life.

Key #5: Gratitude

The ancient Egyptians lived life to the fullest. At festivals and parties, they feasted and drank and were entertained by singers, dancers, and musicians. Children played out in the sun while adults enjoyed hunting, fishing, and board games. Egyptians held feasts to celebrate births, marriages, and religious festivals, or simply to entertain friends. The wealthy enjoyed holding dinner parties at which cooks would prepare huge meals flavored with imported herbs and spices. Dressed in their best clothes, guests sat on chairs or on cushions on the floor, eating and drinking large quantities of wine.

> *"The more you praise and celebrate your life,*
> *the more there is in life to celebrate."*
> —Oprah Winfrey

Most people miss the joy of life. They immerse themselves in fear or pessimism to such a degree that they forget to celebrate even their smallest accomplishments. Life has good moments and bad moments. In the bad moments, we need to shore up our strength, keep our courage, and strive to move forward. In the good moments, we need to learn the art of celebration and gratitude.

Life has a lot to offer and the more you appreciate that, the more you will bring joy and happiness to your life. While scientific proof might not be crystal clear, it is obvious that the universe responds to you the way you see it or expect it to. As Oprah said, the more you praise and celebrate your life, the more there is in life to celebrate.

Train your eyes to recognize the light and beauty of life. Celebrate even the trivial achievements. Make it a habit to see the good and maximize it, and to see the bad—but minimize it. I suggest that you celebrate, every day, the very fact that you are alive. You must celebrate daily the fact that you have a new chance to live your dreams, grow, learn, and prosper.

Think of all the magnificent things in your daily life. Imagine the glorious sunrise, a lush garden, a vast blue sky, mountains thick with towering trees, fragrant forests, a mother's kiss, a baby's smile! Don't deprive yourself of the beauty that surrounds you. Don't take these everyday miracles for granted. Appreciating miracles is as easy as breathing—and even your breathing is a miracle. Think about it. Ordinary people, the ones who see only the dark side of life, live lives of fear, insecurity, and continuous pain. But *you*—you who aspire to be a successful, happy person—you must see the light in your life, the bowl of succulent cherries that awaits you when you open your eyes every morning. And you must develop a sense of gratitude for everything you are blessed with.

Are you happy living a painful life, even when there is simply no reason to? What would happen if you chose to alter your attitude today and to see the magical power of gratitude? What have you got to lose? Be grateful for what you have. Most people only look at the dark side of their lives. They don't see the ocean of blessings that they live in. Being healthy is a treasure in itself. Think of all the good things that you have in your life—and I challenge you to find them anything but endless.

The gratitude attitude is the best thing you can ever develop. When you analyze your life fairly, you'll discover that you have more blessings than suffering. You have so many more good things to be happy about, compared to the small challenges that you might face throughout your life journey. We just got used to focusing on the negative and magnifying it. Just look at your own body—the blessing of having an eye to see, an ear to hear, a tongue to taste, and a heart to feel. You will never be able to count the miracles and blessings that surround you.

Start the good habit of keeping a gratitude journal. Every day before you go to sleep, write down one thing that you're grateful for that day. And believe me, once you begin taking stock of the good things in your life, more good things will be attracted to you. It's as if life rewards you for your gratefulness. Gratitude will open the doors of joy and prosperity in ways you can never imagine. Even if you're in the midst of catastrophe, just think of something you're grateful for and see how the power of gratitude can change everything. Even if doing so may not change your outside circumstances, it will surely change your inner world—your thoughts and attitude—and therefore leave you with total inner peace and satisfaction.

Don't live in an ocean of negativity, grief, pain, and complaints. You're not a victim. You can choose your thoughts. Remember that we create our own experiences. We have control, and the miracles are in our hands. So why don't you create an experience of miracles, instead of adversity and pain?

Break through the blind spot, open your mind and heart, and develop the well-trained eyes that will allow you to see the miracles that already abound in your life. Be grateful and open to the miracle of life.

Follow the pharaohs' code and live your life to the fullest. Celebrate the opportunity you have with the light of every new day to live your dreams and craft your legacy. Live your life in a way that makes this world a place to celebrate and enjoy. Dance with the music of life!

It is obvious that we can't succeed alone. We succeed through others. Others are our customers, friends, families, and communities. By creating a legacy that brings joy to others, we increase our chances of finding our own joy. That is what we are going to discuss in the next section.

Section 3:
How To Create Your Ultimate Legacy

THE THREE GREAT PYRAMIDS OF GIZA,
THE ONLY REMAINING MONUMENT OF THE SEVEN
WONDERS OF THE ANCIENT WORLD

Chapter 9
The Black Magic of Success

"The first concerning the "secrets": all cognition comes from inside; we are therefore initiated only by ourselves, but the Master gives the keys. The second concerning the "way": the seeker has need of a Master to guide him and lift him up when he falls, to lead him back to the right way when he strays."

—Ancient Egyptian proverb written
on the Pharaohs' temples in Luxor

It cannot be denied that success has a certain magic! Everyone wants to become a successful person. But this attractive magic can turn against you if you don't know the truth about creating success—*everlasting* success, that is. If you're sick and tired of the false promises and information overload in the success industry, then you'll be very pleased to read this part of the book.

I'm not going to add another promise, tell you that this teaching is different, or guarantee to give you the (ultimate/hidden/little known) secret that (nobody tells you about/gurus don't want to reveal) that will make you an overnight success. Instead, I prefer to show you in detail why you will fail if you focus on success, and what alternative issues you *should* focus on to build everlasting success and leave a majestic legacy. I'm going to show you an alternative approach that you might want to consider carefully in your quest for success.

And all I want is for you to open your mind and read this part in full without pre-judgment. It will explain itself fully as you go along. One more thing: I want you to wipe the very idea of success right out of your head. Be patient and read this part in full—then you'll see exactly what I mean when I say, "Don't focus on success." What I need you to do now, before we get into the meat of the matter, is to simply stop thinking about success and stop trying to be successful "no matter what!"

My sole purpose in this part of the book is to open your eyes to the fact that *only you* can create your success—and that you can do it without focusing on success or being successful. My goal is to empower you to use what you already have to build the life of your dreams, create everlasting success, and leave a legacy.

The Burning Question

I perceive a big problem that we are so deeply immersed in that we can't even see it. Millions of dollars are spent every year on success literature in all media—books, CDs, tapes, and so on. People are clearly desperate to find the all-in-one remedy, the ultimate cure, the success elixir that will improve their lives. Based purely on the amount of information available, I can readily claim that the success industry is one of the biggest in the world. Massive information overload! Thousands of experts, thousands of step-by-step guides, thousands of promises that your life will change if you try *this* solution.

I am not judging or pointing fingers here, but let me ask you one question: If all this information is available, then *why is only 1-3% of the world population successful? Why are successful people so very rare?* All the tools are there. All the clues for success are there. But most of us are still struggling to find our way. Tell me, up until this very moment, how much money have you spent on success literature? Don't get me wrong—there is nothing better than investing in yourself. But my question is *why aren't you as successful as you deserve to be yet?* With all those experts offering advice, promises, and money-back guarantees that their products will change your life forever, *why aren't you successful yet?* That's the burning question we need to examine.

WARNING #1: There Is No Blueprint for Success

That's my first warning: no one in the world—not even I—can give you a blueprint for success. You will *not* be successful if you follow someone else's blueprint or strategy for success. You are unique, and that means you have to develop your *own* success strategy. You need to let go of the "success blueprint" myth and grab hold of the keys to your own success. Why am I so confident that no one can give you a blueprint for success? The answer is inherent in the question *what is success?*

Consider these points:

- There is no single definition of success. All successful people say that success is different for every person. So what I consider success, you might consider failure, right? Given that, how can I promise you that a single system or blueprint will guarantee your success when I don't know what success means to you in the first place? Make sense?

- You are 100% unique. Every success blueprint on the market lays out the steps that helped its creator to succeed. Therefore, the steps he followed—which are based on *his* character, circumstances, current trends, and specific point in time—are really only valid for *him*. It is not enough to say, "This worked for me, it must work for you." There are hundreds of factors that contribute to the equation. It's just not that easy.

- While there is absolutely no question that there are universal laws of success and general principles, rules, traits, and habits shared by most successful people, the mixture of those elements could never be the same for every person. Every combination lock has the same numbers on it, but each one requires a different sequence to open.

So the bottom line is that only you can decide the best way to reach the level of success you desire. I still firmly believe that successful people have much to offer you and that you most certainly can learn valuable information from the clues they leave behind—but only you can formulate the success strategy that will work for you.

WARNING #2: Focusing On Success Will Only Lead to Failure

Read this carefully and please be patient until I explain:

You will fail if you focus on <u>success</u>. Instead, you must focus on <u>value</u> and <u>service</u>.

If you don't trust me on that one, then hopefully you'll trust Albert Einstein. Yes, one of the most powerful minds in the history of mankind once said: "Try not to become a man of success; rather, try to become a man of value." So what does that mean exactly? It means developing a strategy for your life that is based on increasing your value. It means moving from your current position in life to a different position where you can provide more value better than anyone else.

In fact, all of the success stories that I recorded in my project The Success Avalanche (www.Success-Avalanche.com) share this one common factor. Every person I interviewed focused on service to others, and in so doing increased their own value. And those who serve more people are more successful by default. Want proof? Read on.

Why Bill Gates is the Richest Person in the World

Think about this for a minute. Why do you think Bill Gates achieved such massive wealth? Some common responses to that question might include:

"He is intelligent."
"He is a genius."
"He is lucky!"
"He is the owner of Microsoft."
"He has a product that runs the world!"

If your answer was similar to any of those, then allow me to tell you... *no no no!* Absolutely not! No, I'm not being too harsh on Mr. Gates. I just want to direct your attention to an extremely important concept that will guarantee your success in any endeavor. Simply put, Bill Gates is the richest person in the world because Bill Gates is the most *valuable* person in the world.

One of the major secrets to everlasting success and wealth is the combined power of *value* and *service*. The more you serve, the more you succeed. The more value you add to yourself and to the world, the more wealth and success you accumulate. Bill Gates is making irreplaceable contributions of value and service to the whole world, and he's doing it in a way like no one else. So how valuable are *you* right now? What actions can you take to increase your value just 1%? And what service are you offering to the world? How can you become more valuable by offering more? Answering these questions can transform your way of thinking.

Let's look more closely at the idea of service. Your level of success depends on how many people you help, either directly or indirectly, to become more successful. For example, if what you do helps 100 people to become successful, then you can measure your success by giving it a value of 100. Now you have a numerical factor with which to measure your success and progress in life. And if you want to have more success than you have now, think about how you can help even more people to become successful. When you're at work, help your boss become more successful. Help the team you are working with become more successful. Help your customer become more successful. If you are a boss, look for ways to help your employees become more successful. If you are a father, help your children become more successful. If you are a wife, help your husband become more successful. When all of these people do become more successful, they will transfer that success to their families, their friends, and so on. And right there, you have had a direct and indirect impact on the success of many other people.

So how do you master this powerful combination of value and service? First you must discover your life purpose—the area you have the greatest passion for and in which you can serve the maximum number of people. That area will be your area of greatness, the field in which you can have an enormous impact on others and create a lasting legacy for yourself. Then, instead of focusing on success, focus on specific, measurable activities that will increase your value to yourself and others. Compounded over time, any small effort you make to increase your value will yield a great harvest.

It's enough to remember this simple formula:

Purpose + Value + Service = Everlasting Success

If you apply this idea, you will increase your personal value, achieve more success, make a positive impact on other people's lives, feel satisfied in your own life, and leave a wonderful legacy.

Chapter 10
Unleashing Your Full Personal Power

"The seed cannot sprout upwards without simultaneously sending roots into the ground."

—Ancient Egyptian proverb written
on the Pharaohs' temples in Luxor

I have a story to tell you. Come closer and listen.

Once upon a time, a Chinese student was sitting with his master under an old crooked tree in the forest. The student broke the silence and said to his master, "Master, this tree is very old and ugly. It is of no use. It can't be used for lumbering or to build a house or for any other purpose. It is useless—why don't we chop it down and plant a useful tree instead?" The wise Chinese master smiled and said to his student, "Son, look around the forest. Do you see a tree of better shadow to protect people from the hot, sunny days than this old tree?" The student looked around and with great surprise he said, "No, this tree does provide the best shadow." The Chinese master smiled and said, "That is why this tree is here. You see it as useless only because you want to make something different out of it. Son, everything in this universe is here for a reason, and it is through that reason that its brilliance is fully expressed."

Here is an undisputed fact: like that wonderful shade tree, you are unique. You lose your personal power when you start trying to become someone else. If you are an introvert, you may try to change your essence and become a social butterfly just to please other people. If you excel at a certain sport, you may give it up just because someone told you that a college degree is much more important than being an athlete. And that kind of drama can pervade your life each and every day—the drama of trying to live in the illusion that you would be a better person if you could only change who you really are. But you are what you are because that

121

is how you were crafted to fulfill your purpose. When you overlook your uniqueness and the very reason for your existence, you lose your potential and you lose your personal power.

Take back your power, magnificent person! It is unlimited, and you can perform miracles with it. Just be yourself and listen to your heart. The day you were born, your heart started playing a symphony, the most spectacular symphony ever heard. It is the symphony of your legacy, the symphony of your greatness. Listen to it. Resonate with it. Dance to its rhythms. And unleash your greatness.

Your full personal power is hidden in your heart. It is only when you listen to that music and decide to be yourself that you can change the whole world and discover that there are no limits to what you can achieve. You will only reach your full potential and personal power through effortlessness and by not resisting your own nature and uniqueness. Therefore, be yourself and listen to your heart. Just show the universe the resplendent beauty of who you truly are, and let your symphony play on!

The #1 Success Strategy

Farming and agriculture were central to the ancient Egyptian society and, with the exception of royalty, nobility, and the scribes, most of the population was directly involved with farming in one aspect or another. Members of the nobility were involved on the economic side, as they often owned the farmland and supervised the farming process. The farmers were quite busy most of the year because the growing season lasted between eight to nine months. However, unless a farmer was called up into army service or public works, he did have a period of respite during the flood season. At the height of the floods, usually around mid-August, each farmer would row a small boat around his land and close the vents in the surrounding dykes. Once the Nile subsided, the water would slowly run off, leaving behind all the fertile mud and silt which then soaked down deep into the soil.

The routine of this ancient way of life was perfectly normal—after all, what else should a country with excellent weather, perfect soil, and the legendary Nile River focus on if not agriculture?

So what is the lesson here?

Leverage your natural forces! If you leverage your strengths, your weaknesses will dissolve. That means finding a position in life where you can maximize your strengths and thereby minimize your weaknesses.

Imagine a man who was born with a natural gift for writing, but one day he decides he wants to become a public speaker instead. Unfortunately, he has problems with the tone and clarity of his voice and he stutters. So what does he do? He enrolls in a voice training class to improve his speaking voice and works with a speech therapist to overcome his lifelong stutter—not to mention to overcome his natural shyness. But the result of all this training is that he ends up being just an average speaker.

If this man had instead followed another strategy in which he developed his natural writing talent and strengthened his expertise in that field, the result would have been completely different. And who knows—if he had leveraged his innate gift for writing, he may have won a Nobel Prize some day.

> *"Hide not your talents. They for use were made.*
> *What's a sundial in the shade?"*
> —Benjamin Franklin

Each one of us has at least one special talent that corresponds to our true purpose in life. Don't even think about working on your weaknesses until you master your strengths and position yourself where they can be fully utilized. The moment we try to become someone else just to please others or get attention is the moment we lose our personal power. Instead, apply the #1 success strategy: *strengthen your strengths*. As Peter Drucker, bestselling author and management icon, used to say: "You develop the strengths and you make the weaknesses irrelevant."

You can do that by putting the 80/20 principle into action. The 80/20 principle states that 80% of your results come from 20% of your efforts. Your very special talents and innate gifts constitute 20% of your overall personal skills and traits. So the practical application of the 80/20 principle implies that you need to spend 80% of your effort and time on developing and maximizing your 20% special talents and strengths, because from them you'll achieve maximum results. Leveraging what you already have is the natural and most logical approach to making it big in life.

If your weakness is an issue, then try to find someone to help you with it. For example, English is not my native language and I find it difficult to give life to and draw pictures with my writing. Instead of spending thousands of hours trying to develop my writing skills, I focused on strengthening my expertise and writing down my thoughts as they come to me. Then I found an amazing and passionate editor to work with me and edit every article I write. She gives my writing its solid structure and beautiful rhythm. Together we form a very strong team because each one of us is leveraging his or her own strengths. I have a passion for success wisdom and she has a passion for editing. So we work great together—I get my thoughts on paper and she gives them life and power! And the results speak for themselves.

You can't be excellent at everything. You can only be excellent at the few talents that were planted within you to help you fulfill your purpose in life. If you believe that you were born ready to succeed and fulfill your purpose—that you are already very well equipped with the talents you need to do so—then you will be able to release the ultimate power of *you*.

Johann Wolfgang von Goethe once said: "A really great talent finds its happiness in execution." Find your talents and nurture them, then put them to use. Position yourself in a way that allows you to leverage the natural forces of your environment and trends of the time and follow the path of least resistance to get where you want to go. If you execute your talents, you'll find that you will reap faster and better results, and happiness will follow. The pharaohs leveraged the natural forces of their environment to build the longest-lasting civilization in history. And that is the key to everlasting success, too. *Strengthen your strengths!*

"Argue for your limitations, and sure enough they're yours."
—Richard Bach

How to Liberate Your Uniqueness

Albert Einstein once said: "Few are those who see with their own eyes and feel with their own hearts." If you are satisfied with your life and love what you do, then congratulations—you're one of the few lucky people in the world. But if you are not, you must ask yourself why. The fact is that most people base their opinions and actions on the prejudices and expectations of their social environment. That means that most of us make decisions about our lives based on what other people see, feel, want, and believe rather than on our own beliefs and desires. But the moment you let the opinions of others control your life is the moment you lose your uniqueness—the special quality that makes you *you*. You are one of a kind and you absolutely must see the world with your own eyes and feel it with your own heart.

There are two things you need to do to liberate your uniqueness. First, you must visualize your ideal life. How do you want it to look? Grab a sheet of paper *now* and write down all of the details of the greatest life scenario, of your best life. Then take those details and draw a picture in your mind of your ideal life. Forget about what other people think, or how they've drawn your life for you since your childhood. Decide right now that you will live your life your own way, and in the best way you can. It is never too late.

Second, listen to your own heart. What do you love to do the most? Your *own* passion is the ultimate motivation you need to achieve your dreams and aspirations, and living with passion is the core of a fulfilled life. Following your heart will turn your life into a satisfying masterpiece.

The Million-Dollar Question that Can Unleash Your Full Potential Overnight

Look at the legendary success stories throughout history and you will soon discover that there are no boundaries for human potential. But why can't you unleash *your* potential? Why do you settle for less and keep doing what you've always done? Why are you acting like a bird, going out every day searching for a living, then coming back at night to sleep in your nest?

Here is a simple—yet extremely powerful—question that will expand your mind and expose you to your unlimited potential. Most importantly, this question will reveal to you the top two obstacles that hinder you from unleashing your true potential.

> *What would you do if the universe kicked you out of your nest and took away all of your excuses?*

Imagine that the universe has imposed a magical force on you that gets you out of your comfort zone—your nest—and eliminates all the excuses that you think are holding you back, so that for the first time you can do whatever you want and achieve your wildest dreams. What would you do? How different are you going to live your life? What actions are you going to take? What dreams are you going to pursue? What goals are you going to set for yourself? How confident will you be? It would be like waking up in a new world with unlimited possibilities and opportunities to do whatever you want.

The sad thing is that some people would not even know what they wanted, and that is the true misery of life. So it is extremely important to know what you want and to find your true purpose in life—then you can look for ways to fulfill that purpose and overcome the challenges that you might face. But if you are waiting for the "perfect time" to start pursuing your dreams and finding your purpose in life, then you are sabotaging your chances to act on the opportunities that might appear to you throughout your life. And that is just because you don't know what you really want.

As you can see, the million-dollar question reveals the top two obstacles that hinder people from realizing their full potential.

Obstacle #1: Your Comfort Zone

You get used to your life, accept mediocrity, and settle for less. Why? Because you don't want to go after the unknown. You tell yourself that it's better to stay with what you know and that you couldn't make it big anyway. Take a stand now and get out of your nest. Live a life that is worth living and make your life a masterpiece.

Obstacle #2: Making Excuses

Stop making excuses. Excuses are just reasons for not taking action. They are illusions behind which you hide your laziness. Tell me about a successful person who didn't face challenges along the way. The difference between successful people and failures is that successful people don't make excuses—they take 100% responsibility for their lives.

You have unlimited potential and the best ways to unleash that potential are to get out of your comfort zone and to stop making excuses. Ask yourself the million-dollar question and take some time off *today* to answer it—you will be amazed at the responses you come up with. You will discover a lot about yourself and you will awaken your dreams again. You are magnificent and the world is full of abundance. You just need to believe in yourself and follow your spiritual impulse—your true purpose in life.

So You Think that Life is Unfair

Do you always feel that you deserve a better job, financial position, education, lifestyle, home, car, group of friends? How many times have you thought that life is unfair and that you deserve so much more than you have right now? If you have this feeling frequently then let me ask you this: are you sure that you deserve more?

Spirituality expert Neale Donald once said: "If the whole world followed you, would you be pleased with where you took it?" Set aside some time to think about this important question. If you still think that you deserve more and that life is unfair, then take an even more in-depth look at yourself. You have reached your current level in life based on the quality of your thoughts and decisions and on your personal value and what you can offer to the world. Simply put, you need to work on yourself all the time. Just focus on how to become more valuable to yourself and others. If you do that you will find magic coming into your life. Stop being a victim. Think of the ways this negative mindset might be hindering your success.

You are in charge of your life. Take it from where it is to where you want it to be. Work hard on yourself—that is a habit that will pay for itself. Forget about life being unfair. Do your part first. Improve yourself every day, and then six months from now ask yourself this question again: "If the whole world followed me, would I be pleased with where I took it?" Ask yourself this question every now and then until the answer is yes. Build yourself as if you're going to lead the world.

Next, we're going to discuss five important keys to maximum contribution.

Chapter 11
5 Keys to Maximum Contribution

"True sages are those who give what they have, without meanness and without secret!"
> —Ancient Egyptian proverb written
> on the Pharaohs' temples in Luxor

Increasing your personal value without finding a way to put this value into service is useless. There are lots of businesses that offer a great product but fail in their marketing and sales activities. They fail in making their target market aware of the benefits of their products—and as a result they go out of the market very soon. Your value must be translated into service and contribution. This is a very important skill to learn.

You must know how to work on transforming your value and knowledge into a service that others can benefit from. I consider marketing to be one of the greatest skills that you need to learn whether you have a business of your own or not. Simply put, it is the art of getting your message across to your target market, or the people you intend to serve. In this chapter, I would like to share five keys that can help you increase both your value and your ability to serve.

Key #1: Learning from Success Stories

It is *essential* that you listen to the stories of highly successful people in order to learn how they develop their own formulas and strategies for success. What you'll find is that every story is both the same and entirely different. How can that be?

All those highly successful people had certain things in common. They all had a clear life purpose and great passion for what they do, and they all shared the same ingredients and principles for success. But each one used those common ingredients for success in brilliantly different combinations.

They each mixed those ingredients in their own unique pots and came up with success strategies exclusively tailored to their own needs and desires, their own situations, and their own definitions of success. And you can do it, too.

Once you've discovered your life purpose and identified how you can add value to the world, all you have to do is search for the clues and principles of success that will help you develop *your own success strategy*, a strategy that is based on your specific situation and is as unique as you are.

Success stories are an invaluable tool for helping you understand how success is created in the real world. Why? Because they help you discover the "inner game" of success. You may have already read a lot of success books and how-to information, and perhaps you've gotten an intellectual grasp on some of the success concepts. But just imagine reading a book on how to perform brain surgery. Sure, you could go to medical school and study the concepts and techniques for months, but until you actually get in an operating room and watch experienced surgeons perform the operation, you'll never be qualified to do it yourself. You'll never see how all of the concepts and techniques work together in the real world. That same concept applies equally to creating your own success in life. To be effective, you need to see how successful people have applied the success principles and techniques in the real world.

Here are three easy ways to use success stories to gather the information you need to start developing your success strategy:

1. **Read the Clues.** Search for the common threads that unite successful people. Pick up the clues they've left behind on their paths to success and analyze each one to see if it is useful for you. Keep the ones you like, throw the rest out. If you weave these clues into your own strategy, you'll reach the same level of success they've reached—maybe even greater because you'll be able to sidestep all the mistakes they made.

2. **Discover New Ideas.** Ideas are power. The more ideas you are exposed to, the more you will grow and expand your mind. One idea

can literally transform your life overnight. Keep an open mind and listen to the ideas of successful people. Something you hear may ignite a spark in you today, tomorrow, or ten years from now. File away what you learn so that it will be available to you later in your own success strategy.

3. **Learn Only from the Best.** Gather information only from the most successful people, those who have already achieved the level of success that you aspire to. When you listen to their stories, pay close attention to their thoughts and actions. Examine their tactics, methods, principles, and results. Learning from the best guarantees that you'll have the most pertinent information available when it comes time to create your own success strategy.

The principles, clues, and formulas you'll encounter when listening to success stories are worth their weight in gold. Listening to a personal conversation with a successful person reveals a lot about the inner game of success. But remember—you must take those clues and success formulas and *make them your own.* Success stories can give you all the basic knowledge you need, but you are the only one who can mix and match those basics into a success strategy that will unlock the door to your *own* success—a success as only you can define it.

Key #2: Applied and Specialized Knowledge

At the time of the ancient Egyptians, education was an expensive proposition. Most often only boys received schooling, starting from around the age of five and ending when they reached their teens. If a family couldn't afford to send their son to school, then when he was old enough he would go to work with his father and learn his trade. Schools were usually attached to temples and government offices and children were taught by the priests. Young students learned hieratic script, practicing their writing on broken bits of pottery or wooden boards (papyrus was considered far too expensive to use just for practice!). Older students studied hieroglyphs, math, history, languages, geography, astronomy, and law, as well as gymnastics and good manners.

FACT: Knowledge is power!

Nowadays, formal or self-education can still be quite expensive, but investing in yourself to acquire knowledge is the best investment you could ever make. As Plato said: "Knowledge is the food of the soul."

On one side, people who go to college often don't continue to actively seek knowledge once they've finished their formal education. On the other side, people who couldn't afford to go to college in the first place often think that they have no chance to succeed in life because they didn't have enough education.

Both sides are wrong. Why? Simply because there is a big difference between information and knowledge. Even Einstein once said that information is not knowledge. Education may give you tons of information, but it doesn't necessarily give you knowledge. Therefore, formal education is not enough to succeed in life, and having no formal education simply doesn't matter. What really matters is the *application* of the information received.

Applied information is the true knowledge. As Johann Wolfgang von Goethe said: "Knowing is not enough; we must apply. Willing is not enough; we must do." Information alone doesn't lead to results—if it is not applied, it becomes merely wasted potential. You only achieve true knowledge and wisdom when you apply the information in the real world.

There are an infinite number of information sources available to us nowadays. One is formal education, of course. But there are plenty of other sources, such as the internet, books, audio CDs, DVDs, seminars, and magazines, just to name a few. You can acquire information just about anywhere. But you can acquire knowledge *only* through application and experience. Our friend Einstein also said: "The only source of knowledge is experience."

And then there's the power of *specialized knowledge*—knowledge in its most powerful form. Specialized knowledge is when you have in-depth knowledge of a particular field that you have acquired through years of experience in a very specific niche. You know you have achieved ultimate knowledge when you become the go-to expert in a certain field. And that specialized knowledge makes you the most valuable person you can be. Try *not* to be a jack of all trades.

> *"True teaching is not an accumulation of knowledge; it is an awakening of consciousness which goes through successive stages."*
> —Ancient Egyptian proverb written on
> the Pharaohs' temples in Luxor

It is never too late to acquire knowledge. To maximize your personal value and contribution to the world, you need to acquire information and put it into action. Only then will you have true knowledge and value. And to give your knowledge the maximum impact and power, specialize. Know everything there is to know about a specific niche. Develop as much experience as you can in that one field so that your value will go through the roof and you'll be unmatched. Follow the pharaohs' code and don't hold back from investing in yourself!

Key #3: Persistence
And here lies the answer to why successful people are so rare. It is because very few people have the persistence and patience they need to find the right combination of ingredients to create their success strategies. Some people simply can't overcome the obstacles and circumstances that stand in their way and they quit too soon. But remember this—if you stay in the game long enough, you will find your breakthrough point.

If You Want to Succeed, Go to a Blacksmith
You may be surprised to find out that the blacksmith offers one of the most precious lessons about success that you will ever learn, a lesson that will help you succeed in your own life. Look at the procedure for working with raw metal that every blacksmith follows:

1. Heat the metal until it's red hot.
2. Mold it into the desired form by hitting it with a heavy hammer.
3. Plunge it into a bucket of cold water.

4. Watch the metal crackle in response to the sudden change in temperature.
5. Repeat the process until the metal achieves its perfect shape.

Sometimes the metal can't withstand such harsh treatment and it breaks. The metal has proven to be useless, so the blacksmith throws it away. Now, you're probably wondering what this has to do with succeeding in life. Here is the blacksmith's lesson, a lesson that you *must* engrave in your mind: *In order to succeed, you must accept the blows of life.*

The changes, challenges, and failures you'll experience in your life will mold you into the shape you need to be in and prepare you for success. You must be hard and solid to succeed. Success is never given to the weak. You still have much experience to gain and many lessons to learn before you'll be deserving of the level of success you aim for. And until you've been molded into your best form, you must never, ever give up. If you are unable to tolerate the tough requirements of success, life may find you useless and just throw you away.

The journey to your dream may be long and difficult, but don't lose sight of the rewards. The most euphoric moment of your life will be the moment when you reach the top—the moment when you can finally hear, see, touch, and smell the fruits of your labor, the beauty of your dream, and the value of your legacy.

Persistence is the most important trait you can have and is the key to your success. I can tell you with confidence that you will never succeed without persistence, so heed the blacksmith's lesson and be a rock-solid person. If you are you ready to get red-hot, to withstand the blows of the hammer, to plunge yourself into cold water—then you are ready to sizzle and crackle your way to success.

Edison on Persistence
"Many of life's failures are people who did not realize how close they were to success when they gave up."
—Thomas Edison

Frankly, I was shocked when I read this story: the great Thomas Edison failed 10,000 times before he finally invented the light bulb. And what did he say when someone asked him about that? "I haven't failed. I've just found 10,000 ways that don't work."

Could that be true? How on earth could someone have the patience to fail 10,000 times while working on something that only existed in his imagination? How did he develop that unshakable persistence? Can you imagine the number? He had 10,000 unsuccessful trials. The number is *ten thousand!* Nowadays you see people who quit after their first failure. Haven't they heard about Edison?

Indeed, Edison's example is a perfect illustration of how everlasting success is crafted by persistence and faith. Successful people believe in themselves and their dreams. They have unshakable persistence. Let's have a quick look at Edison's attitude here: "I haven't failed." Successful people don't have the word failure in their vocabulary. To them, failure is a series of lessons. You, too, should remove this word from your vocabulary. Let's face it, you only fail when you quit.

But here is an important question: How can you develop an unshakable persistence that can keep you moving forward no matter how many times you fail? Based on my own personal experience, studies, and the interviews I did with ultra-successful people, I can tell you this: it all comes down to the power of purpose and passion.

When you discover your true purpose in life and the unique reason for your own existence, your inner giant will wake up. You will become unstoppable. When you follow your passion—this energy that fires your soul—you will have unshakable persistence. And that is possible simply because the only way to feel that you are truly living is by following your purpose in life. It is by doing what you love, being a person of value, and making a difference. Your purpose and passion are the unlimited energy source that fuels your motivation no matter how long the journey is or how many times you fail. It is worth every effort from your side to work on discovering your true purpose in life. Ask yourself: "Why am I here? What am I meant to do in this life? What do I love? What am I good at?" I know no other way to have Edison's persistence and create everlasting success.

"Life is like a bicycle. In order to keep balance,
you have to keep moving."
—Albert Einstein

Key #4: Strategic Positioning

As I stressed at the beginning of this section, there are lots of theories and blueprints for success out there, but your own success ultimately depends on you and the unique strategy that you develop. In order to develop your own unique success strategy you have to keep the following in mind:

Success strategy is all about advancing your position over time and making every new position pay. Move into areas where you can provide more value and do it better than anyone else.

Remember what Henry David Thoreau said? "If one advances confidently in the direction of one's dreams, and endeavors to live the life which one has imagined, one will meet with a success unexpected in common hours." So be patient and give yourself time to grow.

Define your purpose and then stay on the road. As you go along, you will find the key to the next step in your journey, and then the next. Every step will have its own key, but as you grow, finding those keys will become easier and easier. Find your niche, your area of greatness, and strive to add value to the world by serving those around you. Remember that success brings more success.

Julia Cameron, an award-winning poet and creativity expert, has said that "growth is an erratic forward movement: two steps forward, one step back. Remember that and be very gentle with yourself." What an amazing truth. Growth is a forward movement which means that you have to know your direction in life. Doing diverse things or achieving success in areas not related to each other is not growth at all.

Growth is about the net result of your efforts. You make two steps forward and one step back but you are still growing because the net result is one step forward. So failure doesn't necessarily mean that you are not achieving your goals. You can fail but you will learn a lesson that will take you toward more success.

When you do make a mistake or fail in something, don't beat yourself up. Do yourself justice by looking at the big picture. Evaluate what you have achieved and you will discover that you had lots of forward steps and that going back for a while doesn't mean that you are a failure. The backward motion is simply preparation for fast-forward steps toward your goals in the future.

Key #5: Intelligent Accomplishments

How do you know that what you're doing in life is worthy and will lead you to where you want to be? You might be an achiever, but if your accomplishments are not linked to a purpose then you're wasting your efforts and your life. At some point down the road you'll stop and ask yourself, "What's next? Why have I been doing all these things in the first place?" And then you'll realize that there's no meaning in anything you've accomplished and that you haven't found that sense of satisfaction and fulfillment you've been looking for. James Allen has said that "until thought is linked with purpose, there is no intelligent accomplishment."

Intelligent accomplishment! That's what you should be striving for. All great achievements in history are built on the collective power of small deliberate actions focused on a single overriding objective. Each accomplishment should build on the previous one, each action should be focused on a sole objective, and each success *must* give your life a sense of meaning and satisfaction. If you don't focus your thoughts and actions, if you don't use your intelligence to work toward your purpose, then your life will be full of empty accomplishments that yield nothing. Wandering aimlessly through life is a weakness that will leave you susceptible to fear and doubt. But having a true purpose will give you strength and make you focused and powerful.

"Thought allied fearlessly to purpose becomes creative force. He who knows this is ready to become something higher and stronger

than a bundle of wavering thoughts and fluctuating sensations.
He who does this has become the conscious and intelligent wielder
of his mental powers."
—James Allen

Once you discover your purpose in life, you'll become a creative force. You'll start to recognize all the opportunities around you and learn to choose those that can move you forward toward the ultimate goal of fulfilling your purpose. There are a lot of choices in life and you'll get lost if you're not clear about your purpose and the path you want to follow. But once you clarify your purpose, you'll become the master of your destiny and take control of your own life. You'll be able to choose the right path for you instead of wasting your time and energy pursuing empty accomplishments that add no value to your life and do nothing to help you create a true success empire.

The smart farmer never throws a bunch of different seeds in the soil with the hope of reaping a diverse collection of fruits. Instead, he focuses his efforts on his clear vision of what kind of harvest he wants. He knows everything about the climate and the earth, and knows which seeds best fit his capabilities and the capabilities of the soil. He knows which crop will bring him the greatest rewards. You, too, must be clear about your destination before you start your journey—otherwise you may cover thousands of miles, thinking you're moving fast and creating success, only to end up in a place that can never satisfy you. And that's when you'll realize that your long journey was full of empty accomplishments—and that, perhaps, everything you'd ever dreamed of had been right around the corner.

"To put away aimlessness and weakness and to begin to think
with purpose is to enter the ranks of those strong ones who only
recognize failure as one of the pathways to attainment. Who
make all conditions serve them, and who think strongly, attempt
fearlessly, and accomplish masterfully."
—James Allen

Start today to develop the power of a laser-beam focus. Think strongly, live purposefully, attempt fearlessly, and accomplish masterfully! Keep advancing your position over time and move into areas where you have maximum value and provide maximum contribution. And remember:

> *"In every vital activity it is the path that matters."*
> —Ancient Egyptian proverb written
> on the Pharaohs' temples in Luxor

Chapter 12
Protect Yourself from the Greatest Tragedy of Life

> *I'm going to die!*

Yes, that is the ultimate truth of life. We are all going to die one day. There are no exceptions to that rule. But you know what? Even with all the sadness that accompanies death, it is not the greatest tragedy of life. Think about this profound pearl of wisdom, uttered by an anonymous person, a person who could have been any one of us and who speaks for all of us: "The tragedy of life is not that it ends so soon, but that we wait so long to begin it."

We wait so long to begin it. We sleep and eat and work and search and search and search. And while we are searching—for what?—life passes us by. Some people never begin to live at all, never discover what it means to live a full life. And *that* is the greatest tragedy of life. A fully realized life can only be a life that we live with passion. It is a life full of energy and spirit. It is a life in which we know who we are and what we are meant to do. It is a life in which we express our talents, unleash our greatness, and explode with personal power. It is a life full of love, meaning, satisfaction, and passion.

That is the quality of life that you deserve to live. And the greatest tragedy of life is that we wait so long to begin living it. Many of us don't realize this truth until we are on our death beds, until it is too late. A lightning bolt splits the sky, electrifying us, jolting us into our own tragic reality—the reality that we didn't live our life as we should and could have lived it. We realize that we didn't appreciate the splendor and possibilities of the life we were given, that we let our fears shape our destiny.

In our last moment on Earth, we are overcome with a wave of regret for what could have been, for what should have been. And the greatest tragedy is that there is no extra time, and there are no do-overs. *Game over*. I am truly sorry for bringing up what are tremendously unpleasant emotions for all of us. But it is important for you to realize that in order to live the life you deserve and protect yourself from this tragedy, you *must* find your true purpose in life and breathe new life into even your wildest of dreams.

You must—right now—stop wandering aimlessly through life without a real purpose. You must refuse to let each new fear wrap itself around you like a heavy iron chain, crushing you under the weight, unable to move, unable to control anything at all. You must start defining who you are and what you want to do with your life. You must remove those chains one by one, imbue your life with new meaning and purpose, and fill your days with focus, passion, and satisfaction. You must have a compelling dream that empowers and motivates you to be and do your best. A dream so worthy that you would die in your path for the opportunity to pursue it. A dream that is your driving force, greater than all your fears and obstacles put together. A dream that challenges you to destroy your complacent reality and to live a fully realized life.

A man named George Moore once said: "Reality can destroy the dream; why shouldn't the dream destroy reality?"

Exactly. *Why shouldn't it?*

So many people suffer so greatly when they realize that their personal reality is destroying their dreams, and they feel powerless to stop it. But all successful people and legendary figures have asked that brilliant, transformational question: Why shouldn't my dream destroy my reality? And that is the seed of *greatness*. That is the seed from which true personal power begins to bloom. What are you waiting for?

Go out and live your splendid life *now*. Don't wait for that bolt of lightning to illuminate the truth when it's already too late to get up and do something about it. Dream big and let your dream destroy your reality. Now is the only time you have to stop, reflect, and think of the difference you want to make and the legacy you want to leave. Now is the only time you have to confront your reality head-on and say:

"Enough is enough! You will not have control over me anymore. I am the greatest. I am crafted for success. I am in charge from now on. I have a dream. I have a dream

that is larger than life. Let me show you what I can do. I love my life, and I will turn it into a masterpiece of light and color and promise. No more fears, no more delays, no more self-limiting beliefs, and no more hesitation. This is my day. This is the beginning of my new life, the life that I truly deserve. Now let me show the world the promise and brilliance of my legacy."

You are magnificent. You are God's most glorious creation. Your power has no boundaries. Go after your dreams, grab onto them with both hands, and don't let go. Put your heart on the line and *live with passion*. And when you come up against the naysayers—those who want to put the chains of their negativity around your neck, who want to keep you from living your dream because they don't want to be left at the bottom to suffer alone—just turn the other cheek. Keep the words of Les Brown close to your heart and "let your best revenge be massive success."

You are ready. Can you feel it? As you open the door to a glittering new life, please take with you this wonderful Indian proverb and know that these words have helped me more than any other advice in my life:

"When you were born, you cried and the world rejoiced. Live your life so that when you die, the world cries and you rejoice."

This is your time. Follow The Pharaohs' Code and transform your life from making a living to making a difference. Find joy in your life and bring it to others. Believe me, there is no better time than now.

God bless you.

To Your Everlasting Success,
Mohamed Tohami

THE MAJESTIC SPHINX AT GIZA

About the Author

Mohamed Tohami is an author and motivational speaker who helps employed professionals transform their lives from making a living to making a difference. He is well known worldwide for his series of interviews with ultra-successful people about their secrets of success, having recorded over one hundred interviews with the world's leading success and business experts like Jim Cathcart, Tony Alessandra, Michael Gerber, Mark Sanborn, and many more.

Tohami is featured as one of the world's top experts in the area of success skills by SelfGrowth.com, the #1 self-improvement site on the Internet. Tohami has also been featured in *Arabian Man* magazine as the Middle East's first self-help guru.

***

If you are dissatisfied with your work and uncertain about your future, and would like to learn more about how Tohami can help you find joy in your life and make a difference, please visit his website at www.Tohami.com.

***

Do you represent an organization that would like to book Tohami to speak and share the wisdom of The Pharaohs' Code with your group?

Tohami can help you build a group of passionate professionals who are making a difference all around the organization. His speeches are geared toward medium and large national companies, multinational organizations, chambers of commerce, and business conferences that are attended primarily by professionals such as engineers, customer service representatives, sales people, marketing coordinators, project managers, administrators, and others. Mohamed Tohami will speak pro bono to charity and non-profit organizations.

If you would like to book Tohami for a speaking engagement, please send him an e-mail at info@tohami.com.

CPSIA information can be obtained at www.ICGtesting.com
Printed in the USA
BVOW08s2038250816

460194BV00001B/53/P